66 GREAT
NAMES AND TITLES
EXPLAINED
AND APPLIED

Who Is Jesus?

PAUL KENT

BA...
An Impri...

Published by Barbour Books, an imprint of Barbour Publishing, Inc., 1810 Barbour Drive, Uhrichsville, Ohio 44683, www.barbourbooks.com

Our mission is to inspire the world with the life-changing message of the Bible.

ecpa Member of the
Evangelical Christian
Publishers Association

Printed in the United States of America.

Contents

INTRODUCTION

Over thousands of years of human history, billions of people have walked this earth. But one stands alone as the most interesting, most inspiring, most important person of all—Jesus Christ.

So who exactly is Jesus?

To answer that question, we go to the most interesting, most inspiring, most important *book* of all—the Bible. It provides dozens of descriptions of Jesus that help us understand just who He is, what He's done, and why He's absolutely essential to our lives.

Of course, the Bible is a large book, written thousands of years ago. Its size and antiquity can be daunting to us, causing us to miss the life-changing truths it shares. That's why we've created *Who Is Jesus?*

In this little volume, you'll find brief entries on 66 great names and titles of Jesus. Each entry summarizes a particular description, giving you a clearer view of one facet of Jesus' amazing personality. Every entry follows this outline:

- IN TEN WORDS OR LESS: A "nutshell" glance at the name or title.

- DETAILS, PLEASE: A longer explanation, incorporating information from throughout God's Word.

- ADDITIONAL SCRIPTURES: One, two, or several other key scriptures.

- WHAT OTHERS SAY: A memorable quotation from a pastor, theologian, or Christian author.

- SO WHAT? An inspirational or devotional thought as a personal takeaway.

Jesus is a person you need to know—the living Son of God who welcomes you into the peace and joy and eternal life that only He can provide. Use this book to begin a journey of discovery that could truly change your life!

ALMIGHTY

IN TEN WORDS OR LESS
Jesus is the all-powerful God described throughout scripture.

DETAILS, PLEASE
Almighty is the first in this alphabetical listing of the character qualities—or "attributes"—of Jesus. And it's one that requires a bit of detective work.

A careful reading of the Bible yields the truth that God, while one Being, is a "trinity" of three persons—God the Father, Jesus the Son, and the Holy Spirit. Each is unique in His person and work, but each is also fully God. (It's hard to understand, but if humans could completely understand God, He wouldn't really be God, would He?)

Many times in scripture, especially in the Old Testament, the term *Almighty* is clearly a reference to God the Father. But the last book of the New Testament quotes "the Lord" as saying, "I am Alpha and Omega, the beginning and the ending . . .which is, and which was, and which is to come, the Almighty" (Revelation 1:8). Is "the Lord" here describing God the Father or Jesus, since verses throughout the Bible refer to both with this phrase?

If you look at the context of Revelation 1:8—that is, what's happening in the other verses surrounding it—you see that the previous three verses definitely describe Jesus, as does the following verse. From that clue, and from other references in the Bible, it seems certain that "the Almighty" is a name not only of God the Father, but of Jesus the Son too.

ADDITIONAL SCRIPTURES
- For unto us a child is born, unto us a son is given: and the government shall be upon his shoulder: and his name shall be called Wonderful, Counsellor, The mighty God, The everlasting Father, The Prince of Peace. (Isaiah 9:6)

- And out of his mouth goeth a sharp sword, that with it he should smite the nations: and he shall rule them with a rod of iron: and he treadeth the winepress of the fierceness and wrath of Almighty God. And he hath on his vesture and on his thigh a name written, King Of Kings, And Lord Of Lords. (Revelation 19:15–16)

WHAT OTHERS SAY

If, after all, the words [of Revelation 1:8] should be understood as spoken by the Father, our Lord's applying so many of these titles afterward to himself, plainly proves his partaking with the Father in the glory peculiar to the divine nature, and incommunicable to any creature. *Joseph Benson*

SO WHAT?

Jesus, who is the Friend of Sinners, Good Shepherd, Great Physician, Hope, Light of the World, Miracle Worker, Redeemer, Savior, and the Way, the Truth, and the Life (all names and characteristics to be discussed later in this book), is also the Almighty God. Whatever He promises to do for you, He has the power to fulfill.

Alpha and Omega

In Ten Words or Less
In modern terms "A to Z," meaning Jesus is everything.

Details, Please
You'll find this name four times in the King James Version of the Bible, all of them in the book of Revelation. Two seem to refer to God the Father (1:8, 21:6), while the others are spoken by Jesus—notably, once in the final book's final chapter: "Behold, I come quickly; and my reward is with me, to give every man according as his work shall be. I am Alpha and Omega, the beginning and the end, the first and the last" (Revelation 22:12–13). Since Jesus created this world (Colossians 1:16–17) and will rule it forever (Revelation 11:15), He is the true Alpha and Omega, the "A to Z" of everything we as human beings are and know.

Additional Scriptures

- For by [Jesus] were all things created, that are in heaven, and that are in earth, visible and invisible, whether they be thrones, or dominions, or principalities, or powers: all things were created by him, and for him: and he is before all things, and by him all things consist. (Colossians 1:16–17)

- There were great voices in heaven, saying, The kingdoms of this world are become the kingdoms of our Lord, and of his Christ; and he shall reign for ever and ever. (Revelation 11:15)

What Others Say
An alphabet is an ingenious way to store and communicate knowledge. The twenty-six letters in the English alphabet, arranged in almost endless combinations, can hold and convey all knowledge. Christ is the supreme, sovereign alphabet; there is nothing outside His knowledge. *John MacArthur*

So What?
Since Jesus *is* the beginning and the end of everything, He *knows* the beginning and the end of everything. Whatever troubles us is completely within His knowledge and power.

Angel of the Lord

In Ten Words or Less
Preincarnate Jesus visited earth as "the angel of the Lord."

Details, Please
Theologians use the term *Incarnation* to describe Jesus' taking on of a human body. Though He is God, He lived among His creation and died on a cross for people's sins. But Jesus had apparently come to earth earlier, as "the angel of the Lord."

In certain cases, the "angel of the Lord" was simply an angel *from* God—but sometimes the angel is identified *as* God. Consider the story of Abraham, following God's order to sacrifice his son Isaac. As Abraham raised his knife, "the angel of the Lord called unto him out of heaven" (Genesis 22:11). This angel stopped the sacrifice, commending Abraham in the words of God Himself: "Now I know that thou fearest God, seeing thou hast not withheld thy son, thine only son from me" (22:12).

Since Jesus said no one has seen the Father (John 6:46), and since the apostle Paul called Jesus "the image of the invisible God" (Colossians 1:15), many perceive these situations as *Christophanies*—appearances of Jesus before His birth in Bethlehem.

Additional Scripture
- The angel of the Lord said unto [Hagar], Return to thy mistress, and submit thyself under her hands. And the angel of the Lord said unto her, *I* will multiply thy seed exceedingly. (Genesis 16:9–10, emphasis added)

What Others Say
The Angel (or Messenger) of the Lord was Himself God's message to us. *Charles Hurlburt and T. C. Horton*

So What?
Jesus' history didn't begin in Bethlehem—He has always existed, and always been involved in the lives of His people.

Apostle

In Ten Words or Less
One sent on a mission—in Jesus' case, saving humanity.

Details, Please
Eighty times, the King James Version uses the term *apostle*. Only once is it applied directly to Jesus: "Wherefore, holy brethren, partakers of the heavenly calling, consider the Apostle and High Priest of our profession, Christ Jesus" (Hebrews 3:1). But several times in the book of John, Jesus says God the Father had "sent" him, an English word deriving from the same Greek root as *apostle*. How was Jesus an apostle? He was sent from heaven to earth on a mission—not to "condemn the world," as he said in John 3:17, "but that the world through him might be saved."

Additional Scriptures
- This is life eternal, that they might know thee the only true God, and Jesus Christ, whom thou hast sent. (John 17:3)

- As thou hast sent me into the world, even so have I also sent [the twelve apostles] into the world. And for their sakes I sanctify myself, that they also might be sanctified through the truth. Neither pray I for these alone, but for them also which shall believe on me through their word; That they all may be one; as thou, Father, art in me, and I in thee, that they also may be one in us: that the world may believe that thou hast sent me. (John 17:18–21)

What Others Say
The twelve were the human apostles of Christ; Christ was the divine Apostle of God. He alone, as sent Son, speaks to us as antithesis to the whole body of prophets (Hebrews 1:1–2). *Daniel Whedon*

So What?
As an apostle of God, Jesus carries with Him God's authority, God's message, and God's power—so we should pay attention to what He says.

Author and Finisher of Our Faith

In Ten Words or Less
Jesus begins our faith, then carries it on to completion.

Details, Please

This phrase appears in the book of Hebrews, where Jesus is described as the goal of our faith journey: "Seeing we also are compassed about with so great a cloud of witnesses, let us lay aside every weight, and the sin which doth so easily beset us, and let us run with patience the race that is set before us, looking unto Jesus the author and finisher of our faith" (12:1–2). An author is a creator, one who originates an idea; a finisher sees something through. So Jesus is behind every aspect of our salvation—no part of it begins with us: "For by grace are ye saved through faith; and that not of yourselves: it is the gift of God: Not of works, lest any man should boast" (Ephesians 2:8–9).

Additional Scriptures

- But ye denied the Holy One and the Just, and desired a murderer to be granted unto you; and killed the Prince [*Author*, NIV] of life, whom God hath raised from the dead; whereof we are witnesses. (Acts 3:14–15)

- Though he were a Son, yet learned he obedience by the things which he suffered; and being made perfect, he became the author of eternal salvation unto all them that obey him. (Hebrews 5:8–9)

What Others Say

You should look upon your faith as a miracle. It is the ability God gives lost men and women to trust and obey our Savior and Lord. It is the ability God gives regenerated men and women to continue to trust and obey. And Jesus is the Author of our faith. *A. W. Tozer*

So What?

With Jesus at the beginning and end of your faith journey, you're in good hands.

Baby in a Manger

In Ten Words or Less
Jesus—who is God—took on human flesh in Bethlehem.

Details, Please
Though "all things were created by him, and for him" (Colossians 1:16), Jesus chose to become like His human creation. He came not as a powerful king, though—rather, as a helpless infant, laid in a manger (a feed box for livestock) when Mary was unable to find proper lodging in Bethlehem: "And she brought forth her firstborn son, and wrapped him in swaddling clothes, and laid him in a manger; because there was no room for them in the inn" (Luke 2:7).

Additional Scripture
- There were in the same country shepherds abiding in the field, keeping watch over their flock by night. And, lo, the angel of the Lord came upon them, and the glory of the Lord shone round about them: and they were sore afraid. And the angel said unto them, Fear not: for, behold, I bring you good tidings of great joy, which shall be to all people. For unto you is born this day in the city of David a Saviour, which is Christ the Lord. And this shall be a sign unto you; Ye shall find the babe wrapped in swaddling clothes, lying in a manger. (Luke 2:8–12)

What Others Say
When [Jesus] was thrown into a stable, and placed in a manger, and a lodging refused Him among men, it was that heaven might be opened to us, not as a temporary lodging, but as our eternal country and inheritance, and that angels might receive us into their abode. *John Calvin*

So What?
The Creator of the universe humbled Himself to experience the human condition, from the point of its greatest weakness. Jesus understands whatever we're going through (Hebrews 4:15).

BELOVED SON

IN TEN WORDS OR LESS
God the Father's term of endearment for His child, Jesus.

DETAILS, PLEASE
On two separate occasions, each recorded by three different Gospel writers, God the Father publicly announced His love for His Son. The first occurred as Jesus began His preaching ministry by receiving baptism from John: "Coming up out of the water, he saw the heavens opened, and the Spirit like a dove descending upon him: And there came a voice from heaven, saying, Thou art my beloved Son, in whom I am well pleased" (Mark 1:10–11). The second time was when Peter, James, and John the apostle saw Jesus "transfigured" (changed into His shining glory) on a mountaintop: "behold, a bright cloud overshadowed them: and behold a voice out of the cloud, which said, This is my beloved Son, in whom I am well pleased; hear ye him" (Matthew 17:5).

ADDITIONAL SCRIPTURES
- Then said the lord of the vineyard, What shall I do? I will send my beloved son: it may be they will reverence him when they see him. (Luke 20:13; a parable describing Israel's rejection of Jesus as Messiah)

- For he received from God the Father honour and glory, when there came such a voice to him from the excellent glory, This is my beloved Son, in whom I am well pleased. (2 Peter 1:17)

WHAT OTHERS SAY
Christ in human nature was matchlessly pure and holy, and in Him dwelt the fullness of the Godhead bodily; therefore was He highly delightful to the Father, and that delight was publicly attested in audible declarations, "This is my beloved Son in whom I am well pleased." *Charles H. Spurgeon*

SO WHAT?
If you want to please God the Father, you need to love what He loves—His Son, Jesus Christ.

Bread of Life

In Ten Words or Less

Jesus is the nourishment that keeps our spirits alive.

Details, Please

In the synagogue of His adopted hometown of Capernaum, Jesus made the claim, "I am the bread of life: he that cometh to me shall never hunger; and he that believeth on me shall never thirst" (John 6:35).

This comment occurred shortly after Jesus had miraculously multiplied five small loaves of bread and two fish into a meal for five thousand men, plus whatever women and children were in the crowd (John 6:1–15). Not surprisingly, the people were impressed—but when they found the Lord the next day, He admonished them: "Ye seek me, not because ye saw the miracles, but because ye did eat of the loaves, and were filled. Labour not for the meat which perisheth, but for that meat which endureth unto everlasting life, which the Son of man shall give unto you" (6:26–27).

When the people asked Jesus, "What shall we do, that we might work the works of God?" (John 6:28), Jesus told them to believe in Him. But they wanted a miraculous sign, like the manna of Moses' day—a mysterious food that settled on the ground each morning after the Israelites escaped their slavery in Egypt. At that point, Jesus declared, "I am the bread which came down from heaven" (6:41).

It's interesting to note that the name of Jesus' birthplace—*Bethlehem*—means "house of bread." The famed nineteenth-century preacher Charles H. Spurgeon said, "Ought not Jesus Christ to be born in 'the house of bread'? He is the Bread to His people!"

Additional Scriptures

- Then Jesus said unto them, Verily, verily, I say unto you, Moses gave you not that bread from heaven; but my Father giveth you the true bread from heaven. For the bread of God is he which cometh down from heaven, and giveth life unto the world. (John 6:32–33)

- I am that bread of life. (John 6:48)

- I am the living bread which came down from heaven: if any man eat of this bread, he shall live for ever: and the bread that I will give is my flesh, which I will give for the life of the world. (John 6:51)

- This is that bread which came down from heaven: not as your fathers did eat manna, and are dead: he that eateth of this bread shall live for ever. (John 6:58)

WHAT OTHERS SAY

Think of His calling Himself bread! How condescending, that the commonest article upon the table should be the fullest type of Christ! Think of His calling our faith an eating and a drinking of Himself! Nothing could be more instructive; at the same time nothing could better set forth His gentleness and humility of spirit, that He does not object to speak thus of our receiving Him. God be thanked for the simplicity of the gospel. *Charles H. Spurgeon*

SO WHAT?

You can have bread in your house, but that only helps you if you eat it. Jesus is the same way—you need to take Him into yourself to gain the benefit.

BRIDEGROOM

IN TEN WORDS OR LESS
Jesus is husband of the church—all who follow Him.

DETAILS, PLEASE

Perhaps you've heard the church described as "the bride of Christ." You won't find that exact phrase in major translations of the Bible, but you'll find the idea. In the first three Gospels, Jesus calls Himself "the bridegroom" without specifically identifying His bride. But the apostle Paul would later tell Christians in Corinth that "I am jealous over you with godly jealousy: for I have espoused you to one husband, that I may present you as a chaste virgin to Christ" (2 Corinthians 11:2).

ADDITIONAL SCRIPTURES

- Then came to him the disciples of John, saying, Why do we and the Pharisees fast oft, but thy disciples fast not? And Jesus said unto them, Can the children of the bridechamber mourn, as long as the bridegroom is with them? but the days will come, when the bridegroom shall be taken from them, and then shall they fast. (Matthew 9:14–15)

- And there came unto me one of the seven angels which had the seven vials full of the seven last plagues, and talked with me, saying, Come hither, I will shew thee the bride, the Lamb's wife. (Revelation 21:9)

WHAT OTHERS SAY

The Bridegroom must come. The true church is His beloved espoused bride. He has waited a long, long time for her to prepare herself for the glad day and to add the last one which will complete the body. *Charles Hurlburt and T. C. Horton*

SO WHAT?

If you are a follower of Jesus, He, as your bridegroom, has taken responsibility for protecting, providing for, and loving you—forever.

BROTHER

We can relate to Jesus on an intimate, familial level.

DETAILS, PLEASE
Jesus had four physical brothers—James, Joses, Simon, and Judas (Matthew 13:55)—but He calls all of His followers spiritual siblings. In a scene captured in three of the four Gospels, Jesus' family tried to get His attention as He spoke to a crowd. Someone told Him, "Thy mother and thy brethren stand without, desiring to speak with thee" (Matthew 12:47). "Who is my mother, or my brethren?" Jesus replied. Then He looked around and said, "Behold my mother and my brethren! For whosoever shall do the will of God, the same is my brother, and my sister, and mother" (Mark 3:33–35). Luke simplified this statement to, "My mother and my brethren are these which hear the word of God, and do it" (Luke 8:21). If we are Jesus' siblings, He is certainly our Brother.

ADDITIONAL SCRIPTURES
- Jesus saith unto [Mary Magdalene], Touch me not; for I am not yet ascended to my Father: but go to my brethren, and say unto them, I ascend unto my Father, and your Father; and to my God, and your God. (John 20:17)

- The Spirit itself beareth witness with our spirit, that we are the children of God: and if children, then heirs; heirs of God, and joint-heirs with Christ. (Romans 8:16–17)

WHAT OTHERS SAY
How wonderful that He [Jesus] should graciously give this title to those who do the Father's will! And what is that will? The acceptance of His Son as our Saviour and Lord, and the submission of our will to His will as revealed in His Word, for His Word is His will. How near and dear He is to us, our Lord and our Brother! *Charles Hurlburt and T. C. Horton*

SO WHAT?
A brother is a friend, a confidant, a protector, and so much more—and that's who Jesus is to His own.

CARPENTER

Before starting His public ministry, Jesus worked with His hands.

DETAILS, PLEASE
Jesus' neighbors in Nazareth struggled to accept the fact that He was teaching them God's truth on His own authority. After Jesus spoke in the synagogue one Sabbath, the people were "offended," grumbling, "Is not this the carpenter, the son of Mary, the brother of James, and Joses, and of Juda, and Simon? and are not his sisters here with us?" (Mark 6:3). Until He began preaching, Jesus apparently followed in His father Joseph's occupation.

ADDITIONAL SCRIPTURE
- And when [Jesus] was come into his own country, he taught them in their synagogue, insomuch that they were astonished, and said, Whence hath this man this wisdom, and these mighty works? Is not this the carpenter's son? (Matthew 13:54–55).

WHAT OTHERS SAY
One of the [early church] fathers preserves the tradition that He "made plows and yokes, by which He taught the symbols of righteousness and an active life." That good father seems to think it needful to find symbolical meanings, in order to save Christ's dignity; but the prose fact that He toiled at the carpenter's bench, and handled hammer and saw, needs nothing to heighten its value. *Alexander MacLaren*

SO WHAT?
Jesus is a king who understands the average person. He was "in all points tempted like as we are, yet without sin" (Hebrews 4:15), and He even performed the same kinds of physical work we do.

COUNSELOR

IN TEN WORDS OR LESS
Jesus brings all the wisdom of God to us.

DETAILS, PLEASE
Around seven hundred years before Jesus' birth in Bethlehem, the prophet Isaiah predicted He would be a "Counsellor": "For unto us a child is born, unto us a son is given: and the government shall be upon his shoulder: and his name shall be called Wonderful, Counsellor, The mighty God, The everlasting Father, The Prince of Peace" (Isaiah 9:6). In the original Hebrew, the term indicates one who gives good advice—but when God Himself gives the counsel, you can be sure it's absolutely perfect.

ADDITIONAL SCRIPTURE
- And there shall come forth a rod out of the stem of Jesse, and a Branch shall grow out of his roots: And the spirit of the LORD shall rest upon him, the spirit of wisdom and understanding, the spirit of counsel and might, the spirit of knowledge and of the fear of the LORD. (Isaiah 11:1–2)

WHAT OTHERS SAY
Wonderful Counsellor: And so Christ is, because He hath been the counsellor of His church in all ages, and the author and giver of all those excellent counsels delivered not only by the apostles, but also by the prophets, and hath gathered and enlarged, and preserved His church, by admirable counsels and methods of His providence, and, in a word, hath in Him all the treasures of wisdom and knowledge (Colossians 2:3). *John Wesley*

SO WHAT?
When you need counsel, Jesus' half-brother James wrote, "If any of you lack wisdom, let him ask of God, that giveth to all men liberally, and upbraideth not; and it shall be given him" (James 1:5).

CREATOR

Jesus made the universe and everything in it—including us.

DETAILS, PLEASE

The first pages of scripture make clear that this earth and everything on it, along with the sun, moon, and stars, were made by God. Genesis 1–2 describe a creation from nothing, simply by the will and word of God—who is presented in the plural. In fashioning the first human, God is quoted as saying, "Let *us* make man in *our* image, after *our* likeness" (Genesis 1:26, emphasis added). The New Testament indicates that Jesus was the member of the Trinity through whom the universe arose.

The apostle John introduced Jesus as "the Word," who "was made flesh, and dwelt among us" (John 1:14). But Jesus has always existed, and was working long before His life and ministry on earth: "In the beginning was the Word, and the Word was with God, and the Word was God. The same was in the beginning with God. All things were made by him; and without him was not any thing made that was made" (John 1:1–3).

The apostle Paul also described Jesus as Creator in his letter to the Christians of Colosse: "For by him were all things created, that are in heaven, and that are in earth, visible and invisible, whether they be thrones, or dominions, or principalities, or powers: all things were created by him, and for him" (Colossians 1:16).

And the apostle Peter made a similar point, briefly, in a sermon he preached in Jerusalem: "The God of Abraham, Isaac and Jacob, the God of our fathers, has glorified his servant Jesus. You handed him over to be killed, and you disowned him before Pilate, though he had decided to let him go. You disowned the Holy and Righteous One and asked that a murderer be released to you. You killed *the author of life*, but God raised him from the dead" (Acts 3:13–15 NIV, emphasis added).

ADDITIONAL SCRIPTURES

- Unto me, who am less than the least of all saints, is this grace given, that I should preach among the Gentiles the unsearchable riches of Christ; and to make all men see what is the fellowship of the mystery, which from the beginning of the world hath been hid in God, who created all things by Jesus Christ. (Ephesians 3:8–9)

- But to us there is but one God, the Father, of whom are all things, and we in him; and one Lord Jesus Christ, by whom are all things, and we by him. (1 Corinthians 8:6)

- God, who at sundry times and in divers manners spake in time past unto the fathers by the prophets, hath in these last days spoken unto us by his Son, whom he hath appointed heir of all things, by whom also he made the worlds. (Hebrews 1:1–2)

WHAT OTHERS SAY

[The apostle Paul] proves Christ to be before and Lord over every creature, more excellent than them all, with a prerogative other princes want [lack], for none of them is a creator of his subjects, who were not made by him or for him, as all creatures without exception were made by and for Christ. *Matthew Poole*

SO WHAT?

If Jesus could create you (and He did), He can *re*-create you (and He will, if you ask). He has the power to correct, fix, heal, and utterly make new all who come to Him (2 Corinthians 5:17).

CRUCIFIED

IN TEN WORDS OR LESS
Jesus died on a cross as punishment for human sin.

DETAILS, PLEASE
It seems grossly unfair that a man as kind, loving, and good—actually, perfect—as Jesus would be killed by crucifixion. But He told His disciples, "for this cause came I unto this hour" (John 12:27). Humanity's rebellion against God demanded the heavy punishment of death, one that God Himself—as the perfect man Jesus—would pay when He was crucified. "Christ also hath once suffered for sins, the just for the unjust," the apostle Peter wrote, "that he might bring us to God, being put to death in the flesh, but quickened [made alive] by the Spirit" (1 Peter 3:18).

ADDITIONAL SCRIPTURES
- Let all the house of Israel know assuredly, that God hath made the same Jesus, whom ye have crucified, both Lord and Christ. (Acts 2:36)

- For the Jews require a sign, and the Greeks seek after wisdom: But we preach Christ crucified, unto the Jews a stumblingblock, and unto the Greeks foolishness; but unto them which are called, both Jews and Greeks, Christ the power of God, and the wisdom of God. (1 Corinthians 1:22–24)

- I determined not to know any thing among you, save Jesus Christ, and him crucified. (1 Corinthians 2:2)

WHAT OTHERS SAY
When Christ died on the cross for sinners, He not only stood in my place, doing what I never could do (forgiving my sin), but He also showed me what I must do if I would save my life, namely, take up my own cross and join Him on the Calvary road of death to self. *John Piper*

SO WHAT?
As the crucified Savior, an old hymn says, "Jesus paid it all." Now, "all to Him I owe."

Desire of All Nations

In Ten Words or Less
Jesus is the leader who will satisfy people everywhere.

Details, Please
The Old Testament prophet Haggai used this phrase to describe the coming Messiah: "I will shake all nations, and the desire of all nations shall come: and I will fill this house with glory, saith the LORD of hosts" (Haggai 2:7). People from every nation want peace and justice, which Jesus will ultimately provide—and His followers will praise the "desire of all nations" throughout eternity: "Lo, a great multitude, which no man could number, of all nations, and kindreds, and people, and tongues, stood before the throne, and before the Lamb, clothed with white robes, and palms in their hands; and cried with a loud voice, saying, Salvation to our God which sitteth upon the throne, and unto the Lamb" (Revelation 7:9–10).

Additional Scriptures
- His name shall endure for ever: his name shall be continued as long as the sun: and men shall be blessed in him: all nations shall call him blessed. (Psalm 72:17)

- And the scripture, foreseeing that God would justify the heathen through faith, preached before the gospel unto Abraham, saying, In thee shall all nations be blessed. (Galatians 3:8)

What Others Say
Jesus is not only the desire of believers, He is the hope of the entire world. As the apostle Paul declared, "At the name of Jesus every knee should bow. . .every tongue should confess that Jesus Christ is Lord, to the glory of God the Father" (Philippians 2:10–11). *George W. Knight*

So What?
Your unfulfilled longings in this world will be satisfied by Jesus in the next.

Door

In Ten Words or Less

Jesus is our access to the Father—and our protection.

Details, Please

Doors serve two purposes—they allow us to enter into a new place, and they also keep dangerous elements out. In John 10, where Jesus identified himself as "the good shepherd," He also said, "I am the door" (*gate*, NIV) for the sheep. He was picturing a protective enclosure called a sheepfold, with Himself as the single opening. "By me if any man enter in, he shall be saved, and shall go in and out, and find pasture" (John 10:9). Only through Jesus can we approach God the Father and find eternal life; and only Jesus can protect us, as helpless sheep, from the threat posed by Satan and the sinful world we live in.

Additional Scriptures

- Then said Jesus unto them again, Verily, verily, I say unto you, I am the door of the sheep. (John 10:7)

- Jesus saith unto him, I am the way, the truth, and the life: no man cometh unto the Father, but by me. (John 14:6)

What Others Say

By Christ, as the door, we have our first admission into the flock of God. By Him God comes to His church, visits it, and communicates Himself to it. By Him, as the door, the sheep are at last admitted into the heavenly kingdom. *Matthew Henry*

So What?

Jesus is your entryway into "life. . .more abundantly" (John 10:10). And once you've gone through Him, you are safe forever. "The good shepherd giveth his life for the sheep" (John 10:11). "I give unto them eternal life; and they shall never perish, neither shall any man pluck them out of my hand" (John 10:28).

EMMANUEL

IN TEN WORDS OR LESS
Jesus is "God with us," the meaning of *Emmanuel*.

DETAILS, PLEASE
This name for Jesus comes from a dual-purpose prophecy of Isaiah. Some seven hundred years before Jesus' birth, Isaiah had told Judah's King Ahaz, whose capital was under siege, that the enemy would not prevail. As proof, Isaiah said, "the Lord himself shall give you a sign; Behold, a virgin shall conceive, and bear a son, and shall call his name Immanuel" (Isaiah 7:14). That was a promise to Ahaz, but the Gospel writer Matthew, under the direction of the Holy Spirit, took the prophecy to another level by applying it to Jesus: "Behold, a virgin shall be with child, and shall bring forth a son, and they shall call his name Emmanuel, which being interpreted is, God with us" (Matthew 1:23).

ADDITIONAL SCRIPTURES
- Abide in me, and I in you. As the branch cannot bear fruit of itself, except it abide in the vine; no more can ye, except ye abide in me. (John 15:4)

- Thomas answered and said unto [Jesus], My LORD and my God. (John 20:28)

WHAT OTHERS SAY
The great secret of our Christian joy lies in this fact, that we believe in a present, not in an absent Jesus; one who is Emmanuel—God with us. *William Nicoll*

SO WHAT?
If you belong to Jesus by faith, you are never alone. God is always with you.

EXAMPLE

IN TEN WORDS OR LESS
The pattern for our Christian lives is Jesus Christ Himself.

DETAILS, PLEASE
It has been said that "children learn best by example"—and there's a lot of truth in those words. The experience of watching another person's life is powerful, and the Bible presents Jesus as the primary example for Christians to follow. When the apostle Paul said, "follow *my* example" (1 Corinthians 11:1 NIV, emphasis added), he indicated that there are mature, experienced believers that we can and should emulate. But the rest of the verse shows that even Paul recognized a higher authority: "as I follow the example of Christ." Jesus' life and teaching are the pattern for everyone who claims His name.

ADDITIONAL SCRIPTURES
- If I then, your Lord and Master, have washed your feet; ye also ought to wash one another's feet. For I have given you an example, that ye should do as I have done to you. (John 13:14–15)

- For even hereunto were ye called: because Christ also suffered for us, leaving us an example, that ye should follow his steps. (1 Peter 2:21)

WHAT OTHERS SAY
The word *example* literally means "writing under." It was writing put under a piece of paper on which to trace letters, thus a pattern. Christ is the pattern for Christians to follow. *John MacArthur*

SO WHAT?
The old question "What would Jesus do?" can be helpful to us in making daily choices—as long as those decisions are based on the full picture of Jesus from God's Word.

Express Image of the Father

In Ten Words or Less
If you want to see God, look at Jesus.

Details, Please
Whoever wrote Hebrews didn't identify himself—but definitely identified Jesus Christ. He is described as the Son of God, heir of all things, captain of salvation—and that's just a sampling from the first two chapters. In Hebrews 1:3, Jesus is called the "express image" (*exact representation*, NIV) of God the Father's nature. What does that mean?

Since human beings cannot see the Father (John 6:46; 1 Timothy 6:16), we need help to comprehend Him—and Jesus is willing and able to assist. As 1 John 5:20 says, "We know that the Son of God is come, and hath given us an understanding, that we may know him that is true, and we are in him that is true, even in his Son Jesus Christ. This is the true God."

Additional Scriptures
- I and my Father are one. (John 10:30)

- Jesus saith unto him, Have I been so long time with you, and yet hast thou not known me, Philip? he that hath seen me hath seen the Father. (John 14:9)

- For in him [Jesus Christ] dwelleth all the fulness of the Godhead bodily. (Colossians 2:9)

What Others Say
In beholding the power, wisdom, and goodness, of the Lord Jesus Christ, we behold the power, wisdom, and goodness, of the Father; for He hath the nature and perfections of God in Him.
Mathew Henry

So What?
If God is daunting—if He seems distant or frightening—remember that Jesus is the "express image" of the Father. Jesus is a friend of sinners (Matthew 11:19) and lays down His life for His friends (John 15:13) because, ultimately, "God so loved the world" (John 3:16).

FAITHFUL AND TRUE

IN TEN WORDS OR LESS
Jesus' trustworthiness toward His people is absolute and never-ending.

DETAILS, PLEASE
The phrase "faithful and true" appears three times in the King James Version of the Bible, each time in the book of Revelation. Twice, it's used as an adjective (see below); once, in Revelation 19:11, it's a proper name: "I saw heaven opened, and behold a white horse; and he that sat upon him was called Faithful and True, and in righteousness he doth judge and make war." The picture is of Jesus battling the devil and his followers at the end of time, removing all evildoing and unveiling "a new heaven and a new earth" (21:1) for His own followers. There, "God shall wipe away all tears from their eyes; and there shall be no more death, neither sorrow, nor crying, neither shall there be any more pain: for the former things are passed away" (21:4).

ADDITIONAL SCRIPTURES
- And unto the angel of the church of the Laodiceans write; These things saith the Amen, the faithful and true witness, the beginning of the creation of God. (Revelation 3:14)

- And he said unto me, These sayings are faithful and true: and the Lord God of the holy prophets sent his angel to shew unto his servants the things which must shortly be done. (Revelation 22:6)

WHAT OTHERS SAY
Notice the attributes of Christ: He is *Faithful*, because He will stand by us to the end. He is *True*, never doing less but always more than He has promised. *F. B. Meyer*

SO WHAT?
Everyone longs for a true friend, someone who sticks with us no matter what. In Jesus, that's exactly what we have.

Firstborn from the Dead

In Ten Words or Less
Jesus' resurrection previews the experience of all who follow Him.

Details, Please
Jesus wasn't the first human being to be raised from the dead—there are Old Testament examples (such as the son of the widow of Zarephath, 1 Kings 17) and occurrences by Jesus' own command, as when He restored Jairus's daughter (Matthew 9), the son of the widow of Nain (Luke 7), and His friend Lazarus (John 11). But each of those people ultimately died again. When Jesus was resurrected after His crucifixion, He was raised to perfect, ongoing life—both spiritual and physical. As the "firstborn from the dead," Jesus is the prototype for all who trust Him.

Additional Scriptures
- And he is the head of the body, the church: who is the beginning, the firstborn from the dead; that in all things he might have the preeminence. (Colossians 1:18)

- John to the seven churches which are in Asia: Grace be unto you, and peace, from him which is, and which was, and which is to come; and from the seven Spirits which are before his throne; and from Jesus Christ, who is the faithful witness, and the first begotten of the dead [*firstborn from the dead*, NIV]. (Revelation 1:4–5)

What Others Say
Jesus' resurrection from death opens the way for all who trust in Him to follow Him in a resurrection like His when He returns. . . . Our ultimate hope is not just for our souls to go to heaven, but for our physical bodies to be raised to new life like Jesus' was. *Justin Holcomb*

So What?
For Christians, death is not the end—just the entryway to richer, fuller life.

FRIEND OF SINNERS

IN TEN WORDS OR LESS
Jesus gladly associates with the "lower classes" of society.

DETAILS, PLEASE
This beautiful description of Jesus was initially meant as an insult. The Pharisees—the picky religious rule-keepers of Jesus' day—thought the Lord's association with tax collectors and other "undesirables" disqualified His claim to righteousness. But they had also criticized Jesus' forerunner, John the Baptist, for behaving in opposite ways. Jesus laid bare their hypocrisy by saying, "John the Baptist came neither eating bread nor drinking wine; and ye say, He hath a devil. The Son of man is come eating and drinking; and ye say, Behold a gluttonous man, and a winebibber, a friend of publicans and sinners!" (Luke 7:33–34). Several accounts in the Gospels demonstrate how Jesus was a "friend of sinners"—for example, His conversation with the oft-married Samaritan woman at the well (John 4:4–42); His calling of the tax collectors Matthew and Zacchaeus (Matthew 9:9; Luke 19:1–10); and His gentle treatment of "a woman in the city, which was a sinner," who anointed Him with oil at a Pharisee's home (Luke 7:37–50).

ADDITIONAL SCRIPTURES
- For John came neither eating nor drinking, and they say, He hath a devil. The Son of man came eating and drinking, and they say, Behold a man gluttonous, and a winebibber, a friend of publicans and sinners. (Matthew 11:18–19)

WHAT OTHERS SAY
Jesus was a friend of sinners not because He winked at sin, ignored sin, or enjoyed light-hearted revelry with those engaged in immorality. Jesus was a friend of sinners in that He came to save sinners and was very pleased to welcome sinners who were open to the gospel, sorry for their sins, and on their way to putting their faith in Him. *Kevin DeYoung*

SO WHAT?
Never fear that you're too bad for Jesus. As a "friend of sinners," He accepts all who come to Him.

FULFILLMENT OF PROPHECY

IN TEN WORDS OR LESS
Jesus' ministry was predicted long before He arrived on earth.

DETAILS, PLEASE
The phrase "fulfillment of prophecy" is a summary statement rather than an actual Bible quotation. But it's a powerful theme throughout Matthew's Gospel, which targeted a Jewish audience, people very familiar with ancient prophecies of the coming Messiah. Here's a key example: "Now all this was done, that it might be fulfilled which was spoken of the Lord by the prophet, saying, Behold, a virgin shall be with child, and shall bring forth a son, and they shall call his name Emmanuel, which being interpreted is, God with us" (Matthew 1:22–23). Additional examples follow.

ADDITIONAL SCRIPTURES
- When [Joseph] arose, he took the young child and his mother by night, and departed into Egypt: And was there until the death of Herod: that it might be fulfilled which was spoken of the Lord by the prophet, saying, Out of Egypt have I called my son. (Matthew 2:14–15)

- And [Jesus] came and dwelt in a city called Nazareth: that it might be fulfilled which was spoken by the prophets, He shall be called a Nazarene. (Matthew 2:23)

- And leaving Nazareth, he came and dwelt in Capernaum, which is upon the sea coast, in the borders of Zabulon and Nephthalim: That it might be fulfilled which was spoken by Esaias the prophet. (Matthew 4:13–14)

- When the even was come, they brought unto [Jesus] many that were possessed with devils: and he cast out the spirits with his word, and healed all that were sick: That it might be fulfilled which was spoken by Esaias the prophet, saying, Himself took our infirmities, and bare our sicknesses. (Matthew 8:16–17)

- That it might be fulfilled which was spoken by the prophet, saying, I will open my mouth in parables; I will utter things which have been kept secret from the foundation of the world. (Matthew 13:35)

- All this was done, that it might be fulfilled which was spoken by the prophet, saying, Tell ye the daughter of Sion, Behold, thy King cometh unto thee, meek, and sitting upon an ass, and a colt the foal of an ass. (Mathew 21:4–5)

WHAT OTHERS SAY

These were not lucky guesses. . .they were precise predictions made by the all-knowing God of the Bible who repeatedly demonstrated that He has perfect knowledge of all past, present, and future events. *Tim Chaffey*

SO WHAT?

A prophecy is a type of promise—so when God fulfills His prophecies of Jesus, we can be sure He'll live up to the other promises He's made in scripture.

Fulfillment of the Law

In Ten Words or Less
As the only perfect human, Jesus perfectly performed God's law.

Details, Please
As with the previous entry, "Fulfillment of the Law" is not an exact quotation from the King James Version, but rather a summary of Matthew 5:17: "Think not that I am come to destroy the law, or the prophets: I am not come to destroy, but to fulfil." Jesus' life certainly fulfilled the predictions of Old Testament *prophets*, but it also perfectly conformed to the Old Testament *law*—both in its moral commandments and its ceremonial demands. Most notably, Jesus Himself acted as the sacrifice for sin. By accepting Jesus' perfect work through faith, we can enjoy the benefit of His fulfilling of the law: "For what the law could not do, in that it was weak through the flesh, God sending his own Son in the likeness of sinful flesh, and for sin, condemned sin in the flesh: that the righteousness of the law might be fulfilled in us, who walk not after the flesh, but after the Spirit" (Romans 8:3–4).

Additional Scriptures

- And [Jesus] said unto them, These are the words which I spake unto you, while I was yet with you, that all things must be fulfilled, which were written in the law of Moses, and in the prophets, and in the psalms, concerning me. (Luke 24:44)

- Philip findeth Nathanael, and saith unto him, We have found him, of whom Moses in the law, and the prophets, did write, Jesus of Nazareth, the son of Joseph. (John 1:45)

- Christ is the end [*culmination*, NIV] of the law for righteousness to every one that believeth. (Romans 10:4)

- Knowing that a man is not justified by the works of the law, but by the faith of Jesus Christ, even we have believed in Jesus Christ, that we might be justified by the faith of Christ, and not by the works of the law: for by the works of the law shall no flesh be justified. (Galatians 2:16)

What Others Say

The Lord Jesus came to fulfill *the predictions of the prophets*, who had long foretold that a Savior would one day appear. He came to fulfill *the ceremonial law*, by becoming the great sacrifice for sin, to which all the Mosaic offerings had ever pointed. He came to fulfill *the moral law*, by yielding to it a perfect obedience, which we could never have yielded—and by paying the penalty for our breach of it with His atoning blood, which we could never have paid. *J. C. Ryle*

So What?

God's law reflects His own perfection, both of which are far beyond human ability. But in His love, the Father sent Jesus to bridge the gap for us. Have you consciously accepted Jesus' work by faith?

GOD

Jesus is not the Father or Spirit, but equally God.

DETAILS, PLEASE

It's hard to understand how Jesus can be both the "Son of God" *and* God—but that's a truth the Bible communicates in three primary ways: (1) the statements of Jesus' followers; (2) the words of Jesus Himself; and (3) the record of Jesus' actions.

His followers were very direct in their declarations. The apostle John, calling Jesus "the Word," said that, "In the beginning was the Word, and the Word was with God, and *the Word was God*" (John 1:1, emphasis added). John also captured the exclamation of the disciple Thomas, when he saw the resurrected Jesus: "My LORD and my God!" (20:28). The apostle Paul contributed to our view of Jesus' godhood by telling the Romans, "as concerning the flesh Christ came, who is over all, God blessed for ever" (Romans 9:5). And the unidentified writer of Hebrews added, "unto the Son he saith, Thy throne, O God, is for ever and ever" (1:8).

Some argue that Jesus never specifically stated that He is God, but His use of the phrase "I Am" contradicts this view (see "I Am" entry, page 45). Jesus also said, "I and my Father are one" (John 10:30) and "the Father is in me, and I in him" (John 10:38). And He told the disciple Philip, "he that hath seen me hath seen the Father" (John 14:9).

Finally, the record of Jesus' actions indicates that He was truly God: He claimed to forgive sins, then backed up His claim with a miraculous healing (Matthew 9:1–7); He raised people from the dead, even predicting and accomplishing His own resurrection (John 2:19–21); He accepted worship (Matthew 14:33, 28:17); and promised people eternal life (John 10:28).

ADDITIONAL SCRIPTURES

- This is he [John the Baptist] that was spoken of by the prophet Esaias, saying, The voice of one crying in the wilderness, Prepare ye the way of the Lord. (Matthew 3:3)

- And they were astonished at his doctrine: for he taught them as one that had authority. (Mark 1:22)

- Again the high priest asked him, and said unto him, Art thou the Christ, the Son of the Blessed? And Jesus said, I am: and ye shall see the Son of man sitting on the right hand of power, and coming in the clouds of heaven. Then the high priest rent his clothes, and saith, What need we any further witnesses? Ye have heard the blasphemy. (Mark 14:61–64)

- And Jesus said unto him, Why callest thou me good? none is good, save one, that is, God. (Luke 18:19)

- In your relationships with one another, have the same mindset as Christ Jesus: Who, being in very nature God, did not consider equality with God something to be used to his own advantage. (Philippians 2:5–6 NIV)

- We wait for the blessed hope—the appearing of the glory of our great God and Savior, Jesus Christ. (Titus 2:13 NIV)

WHAT OTHERS SAY

I believe. . .in one Lord Jesus Christ, the only-begotten Son of God. . .God of God, Light of Light, very God of very God; begotten, not made, being of one substance with the Father. *The Nicene Creed*

SO WHAT?

If God is the all-powerful, all-knowing Creator of the universe, if Jesus is truly God, and if you have accepted His salvation by faith, you are completely protected and provided for. There is no need for worry or stress!

Good Shepherd

In Ten Words or Less
Jesus guides, protects, and provides for His "sheep"—human followers.

Details, Please
It's not surprising that Jesus, called the "son [descendant] of David" (Luke 18:38; Mark 12:35), would draw upon one of David's most famous and enduring images to describe Himself. In Psalm 23, David wrote, "The Lord is my shepherd." Jesus elaborated on that idea by twice calling Himself the "good shepherd." What makes Him so good is that He "giveth his life for the sheep" (John 10:11), or more personally, "I lay down my life for the sheep" (John 10:15). This imagery of God as shepherd is common throughout scripture, in the Psalms, the prophets, the Gospels, and the New Testament letters.

Additional Scriptures
- And I will set up one shepherd over them, and he shall feed them, even my servant David; he shall feed them, and he shall be their shepherd. (Ezekiel 34:23)

- But when [Jesus] saw the multitudes, he was moved with compassion on them, because they fainted, and were scattered abroad, as sheep having no shepherd. (Matthew 9:36)

- When the Son of man shall come in his glory, and all the holy angels with him, then shall he sit upon the throne of his glory: And before him shall be gathered all nations: and he shall separate them one from another, as a shepherd divideth his sheep from the goats. (Matthew 25:31–32)

- Then saith Jesus unto them, All ye shall be offended because of me this night: for it is written, I will smite the shepherd, and the sheep of the flock shall be scattered abroad. (Matthew 26:31)

- And Jesus, when he came out, saw much people, and was moved with compassion toward them, because they were as sheep not having a shepherd: and he began to teach them many things. (Mark 6:34)

- Now the God of peace, that brought again from the dead our Lord Jesus, that great shepherd of the sheep, through the blood of the everlasting covenant, make you perfect in every good work to do his will. (Hebrews 13:20–21)

- And when the chief Shepherd shall appear, ye shall receive a crown of glory that fadeth not away. (1 Peter 5:4)

What Others Say

Jesus Christ is the best of shepherds, the best in the world to take the oversight of souls, none so skillful, so faithful, so tender, as He, no such feeder and leader, no such protector and healer of souls as He. *Matthew Henry*

So What?

If your life belongs to Jesus, you're not only in good hands—you're protected by the almighty God of the universe.

GREAT HIGH PRIEST

IN TEN WORDS OR LESS
Jesus is the one true mediator between God and man.

DETAILS, PLEASE
This phrase appears only in Hebrews 4:14—"Seeing then that we have a great high priest, that is passed into the heavens, Jesus the Son of God, let us hold fast our profession." But Hebrews calls Jesus our "high priest" ten other times. In ancient Israel, priests were God's ministers to the everyday people, and high priests were the most important ones—only they could enter God's presence on the annual day of atonement. While they were fallible humans like everyone else, Jesus is perfect—truly the "great" high priest for all people, of all time.

ADDITIONAL SCRIPTURES
- Wherefore in all things it behoved [Jesus] to be made like unto his brethren, that he might be a merciful and faithful high priest in things pertaining to God, to make reconciliation for the sins of the people. (Hebrews 2:17)
- Wherefore, holy brethren, partakers of the heavenly calling, consider the Apostle and High Priest of our profession, Christ Jesus. (Hebrews 3:1)
- For we have not an high priest which cannot be touched with the feeling of our infirmities; but was in all points tempted like as we are, yet without sin. (Hebrews 4:15)

WHAT OTHERS SAY
We have a great High Priest, Jesus Christ, who came into the world as the Son of God, lived a sinless life, offered Himself as a perfect sacrifice for the sins of his people, rose to everlasting life at the right hand of the majesty of God, and there loves us and prays for us and bids us draw near to God through Him. He did not come to fit into the old system of priestly sacrifices. He came to fulfill them and end them. *John Piper*

SO WHAT?
If you are "in Christ," you enjoy His full support in approaching the Father.

Great Physician

In Ten Words or Less
Jesus is a healer of both physical and spiritual sickness.

Details, Please
You won't find this exact phrase in your Bible, but it's an appropriate description of Jesus' capability in healing the body and spirit. The Lord often healed people's physical diseases and infirmities—for example, the fever of Peter's mother-in-law (Matthew 8:14–15); a skin disease called leprosy (Luke 17:11–19); and a man's "withered hand" (Matthew 12:10–13). In fact, Jesus often healed the masses of people who followed Him around: "And his fame went throughout all Syria: and they brought unto him all sick people that were taken with divers diseases and torments, and those which were possessed with devils, and those which were lunatick, and those that had the palsy; and he healed them" (Matthew 4:24; see also Matthew 12:15, 14:14; Luke 5:15). Luke 9:11 mentions these large-scale physical healings that Jesus performed, but adds the important element of spiritual healing, as well: "And the people, when they knew it, followed him: and he received them, *and spake unto them of the kingdom of God,* and healed them that had need of healing" (emphasis added).

This was Jesus' real mission on earth, the one He made plain to the proud Pharisees who grumbled that He associated with "sinful" people: "And it came to pass, that, as Jesus sat at meat in his house, many publicans and sinners sat also together with Jesus and his disciples: for there were many, and they followed him. And when the scribes and Pharisees saw him eat with publicans and sinners, they said unto his disciples, How is it that he eateth and drinketh with publicans and sinners? When Jesus heard it, he saith unto them, They that are whole have no need of the physician, but they that are sick: I came not to call the righteous, but sinners to repentance" (Mark 2:15–17).

Additional Scriptures
- Bless the LORD, O my soul, and forget not all his benefits: Who forgiveth all thine iniquities; who healeth all thy diseases; Who redeemeth thy life from destruction. (Psalm 103:2–4)

- Who his own self bare our sins in his own body on the tree, that we, being dead to sins, should live unto righteousness: by whose stripes ye were healed. (1 Peter 2:24)

WHAT OTHERS SAY

The Lord Jesus came into the world to be a physician as well as a teacher. He knew the necessities of human nature. He saw us all sick of a mortal disease, stricken with the plague of sin, and dying daily. He pitied us, and came down to bring divine medicine for our relief. He came to give health and cure to the dying, to heal the broken hearted, and to offer strength to the weak. No sin-sick soul is too far gone for Him. *J. C. Ryle*

SO WHAT?

There is no weakness, pain, or disability in our lives beyond the healing power of the Great Physician.

HEAD OF THE CHURCH

IN TEN WORDS OR LESS
Jesus is the guiding life force of His people.

DETAILS, PLEASE
Among the higher forms of life, a body needs a head to function. This is true of the Christian church as well. The apostle Paul described all the followers of Jesus as a single body that "hath many members" (1 Corinthians 12:12)—eyes and ears and hands and feet can be likened to the preachers, teachers, administrators, and workers who make the church work. Leading and guiding and providing life for that body is the head, Jesus Christ. As Paul wrote elsewhere, "The husband is the head of the wife, even as Christ is the head of the church: and he is the saviour of the body" (Ephesians 5:23).

ADDITIONAL SCRIPTURES
- [God] hath put all things under [Jesus'] feet, and gave him to be the head over all things to the church, which is his body, the fulness of him that filleth all in all. (Ephesians 1:22–23)
- And he is the head of the body, the church: who is the beginning, the firstborn from the dead; that in all things he might have the preeminence. (Colossians 1:18)

WHAT OTHERS SAY
The constitution of the body will be in a right state, if simply the Head, which furnishes the several members with everything that they have, is allowed, without any hinderance, to have the pre-eminence. *John Calvin*

SO WHAT?
With Jesus as the head, life becomes easier. "Trust in the LORD with all thine heart; and lean not unto thine own understanding. In all thy ways acknowledge him, and he shall direct thy paths" (Proverbs 3:5–6).

Hope

In Ten Words or Less

For everyone in Christ, there is always confidence and expectation.

Details, Please

Jesus as our hope was an ongoing theme in the apostle Paul's writings: "Christ in you, the hope of glory" (Colossians 1:27); "Jesus Christ, which is our hope" (1 Timothy 1:1); "that blessed hope, and the glorious appearing of. . .our Saviour Jesus Christ" (Titus 2:13). But other New Testament writers also picked up the theme. Peter: "Hope to the end for the grace that is to be brought unto you at the revelation of Jesus Christ" (1 Peter 1:13); John: "When [Jesus] shall appear, we shall be like him. . . . And every man that hath this hope in him purifieth himself" (1 John 3:2–3); the author of Hebrews: "Which hope we have as an anchor of the soul, both sure and stedfast, and which entereth into that within the veil; whither the forerunner is for us entered, even Jesus" (Hebrews 6:19–20).

Additional Scriptures

- I would not have you to be ignorant, brethren, concerning them which are asleep, that ye sorrow not, even as others which have no hope. For if we believe that Jesus died and rose again, even so them also which sleep in Jesus will God bring with him. (1 Thessalonians 4:13–14)

What Others Say

As we are even here on earth united with Christ through faith and are partakers of all His blessings and gifts, thus we also have the certain confidence of attaining to the end of our faith, the salvation of our souls. *Paul Kretzmann*

So What?

Life may be hard, but for the Christian, it is never hopeless. Because of Jesus, there is always the promise of a better day—even if that's in eternity.

I Am

In Ten Words or Less

Jesus applied God's unique Old Testament name to Himself.

Details, Please

In the Gospel of John, we find seven "I am" statements of Jesus, comments He made to define Himself to His hearers. You can see those powerful statements in the "Additional Scriptures" section below. But Jesus also spoke the phrase "I Am" by itself, without an object, echoing the name by which God identified Himself to Moses: "Thus shalt thou say unto the children of Israel, I Am hath sent me unto you" (Exodus 3:14). In John 8:58, during an argument with the Jewish scribes and Pharisees, Jesus proclaimed His superiority to their beloved patriarch: "Before Abraham was, *I am*" (emphasis added). This statement clearly implied Jesus' oneness with God the Father. The religious leaders, who jealously guarded what they believed to be God's honor, wanted to stone Jesus to death for blasphemy (John 8:59). But since it was not His time to die, He escaped the angry crowd. Later, as the perfect God-man, Jesus would submit to death on a cross as payment for human sin.

Additional Scriptures

- And Jesus said unto them, I am the bread of life: he that cometh to me shall never hunger; and he that believeth on me shall never thirst. (John 6:35)

- Then spake Jesus again unto them, saying, I am the light of the world: he that followeth me shall not walk in darkness, but shall have the light of life. (John 8:12)

- I am the door: by me if any man enter in, he shall be saved, and shall go in and out, and find pasture. (John 10:9)

- I am the good shepherd: the good shepherd giveth his life for the sheep. (John 10:11)

- Jesus said unto her, I am the resurrection, and the life: he that believeth in me, though he were dead, yet shall he live. (John 11:25)

- Jesus saith unto him, I am the way, the truth, and the life: no man cometh unto the Father, but by me. (John 14:6)

- I am the vine, ye are the branches: He that abideth in me, and I in him, the same bringeth forth much fruit: for without me ye can do nothing. (John 15:5)

WHAT OTHERS SAY

When Jesus took on God's holy title as His own, He was stating the modern equivalent of "I am God." He did this repeatedly over the course of his ministry (see Mark 14:62, John 18:5–6, John 8:24 and John 8:28). So while you may not find the expression "I am God" in the Gospels, you'll certainly find the ancient equivalent. *J. Warner Wallace*

SO WHAT?

If you have any doubt about who Jesus is—whether He's simply a good moral teacher or something more—this name settles the debate: Jesus is God, the second person of the Trinity, absolutely capable of helping you through any difficulty you face. And because He died on the cross for you, He's absolutely willing, as well.

Jesus

Jesus is the personal name of the Trinity's second member.

Details, Please

This name appears in 942 verses in the King James Version of the Bible. The earliest in time—Luke 1:31—provides context for all of the others. When the angel Gabriel visited the virgin Mary in the town of Nazareth, he told her, "Thou shalt conceive in thy womb, and bring forth a son, and shalt call his name Jesus" (Luke 1:31). *Jesus* comes from a Greek adaptation of *Joshua*, the Old Testament name meaning "Jehovah is salvation." The prophet Isaiah had proclaimed that "all the ends of the earth shall see the salvation of our God" (52:10), and the apostle John's vision of heaven in the last days included individuals "of all nations, and kindreds, and people, and tongues" shouting praise for the salvation Jesus provides (Revelation 7:9–11).

Additional Scriptures

- And when eight days were accomplished for the circumcising of the child, his name was called Jesus, which was so named of the angel before he was conceived in the womb. (Luke 2:21)

- For there is one God, and one mediator between God and men, the man Christ Jesus. (1 Timothy 2:5)

What Others Say

Ever since the first Christmas, *Jesus* has been more than just a name. It's been our only comfort in life and in death, our only hope in a hopeless world. *Kevin DeYoung*

So What?

Jesus is a personal name, and He is a personal God. He will hear any time you call His name.

Judge

IN TEN WORDS OR LESS
Perfect justice will be served by the all-knowing, all-powerful Jesus.

DETAILS, PLEASE

Many people, even those who don't claim to follow Jesus, like to repeat His words, "Judge not, that ye be not judged" (Matthew 7:1). In the context, He was denouncing hypocrisy, the way we human beings tend to criticize other people for the sins that we ourselves commit. Since Jesus never sinned (Hebrews 4:15), He has the right and authority to judge the people He created—and He will do so with perfect knowledge and accuracy. The apostle Paul called Jesus "the righteous judge" (2 Timothy 4:8), who will review both "the quick and the dead" (2 Timothy 4:1)—every human being of all time—when He sets up His eternal kingdom. That is the time, according to Paul, "when God shall judge the secrets of men by Jesus Christ according to my gospel" (Romans 2:16). What secrets? Most importantly, whether each individual has trusted in Jesus for salvation.

ADDITIONAL SCRIPTURES

- For the Father judgeth no man, but hath committed all judgment unto the Son. (John 5:22)

- I [Jesus] can of mine own self do nothing: as I hear, I judge: and my judgment is just; because I seek not mine own will, but the will of the Father which hath sent me. (John 5:30)

- Ye judge after the flesh; I judge no man. And yet if I judge, my judgment is true: for I am not alone, but I and the Father that sent me. (John 8:15–16)

- And if any man hear my words, and believe not, I judge him not: for I came not to judge the world, but to save the world. He that rejecteth me, and receiveth not my words, hath one that judgeth him: the word that I have spoken, the same shall judge him in the last day. For I have not spoken of myself; but the Father which sent me, he gave me a commandment, what I should say, and what I should speak. (John 12:47–49)

- And he commanded us to preach unto the people, and to testify that it is he which was ordained of God to be the Judge of quick and dead. (Acts 10:42)

- Because [God] hath appointed a day, in the which he will judge the world in righteousness by that man whom he hath ordained; whereof he hath given assurance unto all men, in that he hath raised him from the dead. (Acts 17:31)

- Therefore judge nothing before the time, until the Lord come, who both will bring to light the hidden things of darkness, and will make manifest the counsels of the hearts: and then shall every man have praise of God. (1 Corinthians 4:5)

- And I saw heaven opened, and behold a white horse; and he that sat upon him was called Faithful and True, and in righteousness he doth judge and make war. (Revelation 19:11)

WHAT OTHERS SAY

Nothing speaks more terror to sinners, or more comfort to saints, than this, that Christ shall be the Judge. *Matthew Henry*

SO WHAT?

Deep down, we know we're accountable to God for our sin. But through Jesus, we all have the opportunity to be forgiven—and when judgment day comes, we can rest assured that His perfection covers every one of our failures.

King of Kings

In Ten Words or Less
Jesus exceeds every other ruler in royalty and power.

Details, Please
In the Old Testament, the Persian ruler Artaxerxes called himself "king of kings" (Ezra 7:12), indicating his supremacy over the lesser rulers he had conquered. God Himself even called the Babylonian leader Nebuchadnezzar "king of kings" in Ezekiel 26:7. But these "kings of kings" were limited in time and place, with a power that only hinted at the ultimate Ruler of all, Jesus Christ. As John described Him in the book of Revelation, "Out of his mouth goeth a sharp sword, that with it he should smite the nations: and he shall rule them with a rod of iron: and he treadeth the winepress of the fierceness and wrath of Almighty God. And he hath on his vesture and on his thigh a name written, KING OF KINGS, AND LORD OF LORDS" (19:15–16).

Additional Scripture
- These shall make war with the Lamb, and the Lamb shall overcome them: for he is Lord of lords, and King of kings: and they that are with him are called, and chosen, and faithful. (Revelation 17:14)

What Others Say
Great sovereigns, like those of Persia, who had kings and viceroys for their vassals, were accustomed to display this title. But none but He who here wears it is entitled to its universal extent. *Daniel Whedon*

So What?
If you're a believer, you serve the highest Authority of all. Every king or queen or president or prime minister ultimately reports to Jesus, who loved you to the death.

KING OF THE JEWS

IN TEN WORDS OR LESS
Jesus, the King of kings, also rules His particular people.

DETAILS, PLEASE
This name was assigned to Jesus, shortly after His birth and just before His death. "Where is he that is born King of the Jews?" wise men from the east asked in Jerusalem (Matthew 2:2). Thirty-some years later, also in Jerusalem, it was the Roman governor Pilate using the phrase. "And Jesus stood before the governor: and the governor asked him, saying, Art thou the King of the Jews? And Jesus said unto him, Thou sayest" (Matthew 27:11). Roman soldiers repeated the name to mock their prisoner (Matthew 27:29). And shortly thereafter, "King of the Jews" would be written, in three languages, on a sign affixed to Jesus' cross.

ADDITIONAL SCRIPTURES
- But Pilate answered them, saying, Will ye that I release unto you the King of the Jews? (Mark 15:9)

- And the superscription of his accusation was written over, THE KING OF THE JEWS. (Mark 15:26)

- Then said the chief priests of the Jews to Pilate, Write not, The King of the Jews; but that he said, I am King of the Jews. Pilate answered, What I have written I have written. (John 19:21–22)

WHAT OTHERS SAY
Though [Pilate's] motive probably was to ridicule the Savior, yet the thing was done as God would have it—and Jesus on the cross hung there proclaimed by Roman authority as "the King of the Jews." *Charles Spurgeon*

SO WHAT?
Few Jews have acknowledged Jesus as their king—but you can and should.

Lamb of God

In Ten Words or Less
Jesus was the one perfect sacrifice for human sin.

Details, Please
John the Baptist used this phrase, which appears twice in the first chapter of the apostle John's Gospel: "John seeth Jesus coming unto him, and saith, Behold the Lamb of God, which taketh away the sin of the world" (1:29); "And looking upon Jesus as he walked, he saith, Behold the Lamb of God!" (1:36). The references hark back to the Israelites' escape from slavery in Egypt, when God told them to slaughter a lamb and daub its blood on the doorposts of their homes. God promised, "When I see the blood, I will pass over you, and the plague shall not be upon you to destroy you, when I smite the land of Egypt" (Exodus 12:13). That pictured the way He would deal with the people who are covered by Jesus' blood shed on the cross—they will be protected from God's wrath over sin.

Additional Scriptures
- Forasmuch as ye know that ye were not redeemed with corruptible things, as silver and gold, from your vain conversation received by tradition from your fathers; but with the precious blood of Christ, as of a lamb without blemish and without spot. (1 Peter 1:18–19)

- And I beheld, and I heard the voice of many angels round about the throne and the beasts and the elders: and the number of them was ten thousand times ten thousand, and thousands of thousands; saying with a loud voice, Worthy is the Lamb that was slain to receive power, and riches, and wisdom, and strength, and honour, and glory, and blessing. (Revelation 5:11–12)

- After this I beheld, and, lo, a great multitude, which no man could number, of all nations, and kindreds, and people, and tongues, stood before the throne, and before the Lamb, clothed with white robes, and palms in their hands; and cried with a loud voice, saying, Salvation to our God which sitteth upon the throne, and unto the Lamb. (Revelation 7:9–10)

- These shall make war with the Lamb, and the Lamb shall overcome them: for he is Lord of lords, and King of kings: and they that are with him are called, and chosen, and faithful. (Revelation 17:14)

WHAT OTHERS SAY

It is our duty, with an eye of faith, to *behold* the Lamb of God thus taking away the *sin of the world*. See Him taking away sin, and let that increase our hatred of sin, and resolutions against it. Let not us hold that fast which the Lamb of God came to take away: for Christ will either take our sins away or take us away. *Matthew Henry*

SO WHAT?

We all have a problem—sin—and we can all "behold" the solution: Jesus, the Lamb of God. His sacrifice covers everyone who turns to Him in humble faith.

Last Adam

In Ten Words or Less
Physical life comes through Adam; spiritual life through Jesus Christ.

Details, Please
In 1 Corinthians 15, the classic passage on resurrection, the apostle Paul uses a title for Jesus that appears nowhere else in scripture: "And so it is written, The first man Adam was made a living soul; the last Adam was made a quickening spirit" (verse 45). Basically, Paul argued, human beings derive their physical life—and death—from the first human being, Adam. But Jesus is a new Adam, the "last Adam," who provides *spiritual* life—and, ultimately, a new physical body that will last forever.

Additional Scriptures
- For as in Adam all die, even so in Christ shall all be made alive. (1 Corinthians 15:22)
- For God so loved the world, that he gave his only begotten Son, that whosoever believeth in him should not perish, but have everlasting life. (John 3:16)

What Others Say
The image of the first man we have by our natural and physical derivation from him, the image of the second by spiritual derivation; that is to say, by our choosing Christ as our ideal and by our allowing His Spirit to form us. This Spirit is life giving; this Spirit is indeed God, communicating to us a life which is at once holy and eternal. *William Nicoll*

So What?
Human beings are automatically members of Adam's dysfunctional family—but adoption into the family of God requires a choice. Have you "received" Jesus by faith (John 1:12)?

LIGHT OF THE WORLD

IN TEN WORDS OR LESS
By Jesus, we can "see" the reality of God's truth.

DETAILS, PLEASE
The Bible uses the word *light* in both a physical and a spiritual sense. Genesis 1:3 reflects the former: "And God said, Let there be light: and there was light." John 8:12 addresses the latter: "Then spake Jesus again unto them, saying, I am the light of the world: he that followeth me shall not walk in darkness, but shall have the light of life." Just as physical light allows our physical eyes to perceive physical things, Jesus—as "the light of the world"—allows our spiritual eyes to perceive spiritual truths. Without Jesus, as the apostle Paul wrote, "the god of this world hath blinded the minds of them which believe not, lest the light of the glorious gospel of Christ, who is the image of God, should shine unto them" (2 Corinthians 4:4).

ADDITIONAL SCRIPTURES
- [Simeon said of the baby Jesus,] Mine eyes have seen thy salvation, which thou hast prepared before the face of all people; a light to lighten the Gentiles, and the glory of thy people Israel. (Luke 2:30–32)

- In him was life; and the life was the light of men. (John 1:4)

- [John the Baptist] came for a witness, to bear witness of the Light, that all men through him might believe. He was not that Light, but was sent to bear witness of that Light. That was the true Light, which lighteth every man that cometh into the world. (John 1:7–9)

- As long as I am in the world, I am the light of the world. (John 9:5)

- I am come a light into the world, that whosoever believeth on me should not abide in darkness. (John 12:46)

- . . .that Christ should suffer, and that he should be the first that should rise from the dead, and should shew light unto the people, and to the Gentiles. (Acts 26:23)

- God, who commanded the light to shine out of darkness, hath shined in our hearts, to give the light of the knowledge of the glory of God in the face of Jesus Christ. (2 Corinthians 4:6)

- Wherefore he saith, Awake thou that sleepest, and arise from the dead, and Christ shall give thee light. (Ephesians 5:14)

- And the city [new Jerusalem] had no need of the sun, neither of the moon, to shine in it: for the glory of God did lighten it, and the Lamb is the light thereof. (Revelation 21:23)

WHAT OTHERS SAY

Jesus' being "the light of the world" means the world has no other light than Him. If there is going to be a light for the world, it will be Jesus. It is Jesus or darkness. There is no third alternative. No other light. *John Piper*

SO WHAT?

If you're feeling "in the dark," there is an answer: follow Jesus. When you do, He promised in John 8:12, you "*shall have* the light of life."

LORD

IN TEN WORDS OR LESS

Jesus has power, authority, and control over everyone and everything.

DETAILS, PLEASE

The Greek word translated "lord" in the King James New Testament indicates power and authority, and is used to honor a wide variety of individuals, including owners, masters, kings, husbands, and even angels. But when applied to Jesus, "Lord" represents the Old Testament names of God and implies supreme power and authority. In his sermon on the day of Pentecost, Peter saw three thousand people believe in Jesus after he declared, "Therefore let all the house of Israel know assuredly, that God hath made the same Jesus, whom ye have crucified, both Lord and Christ" (Acts 2:36).

ADDITIONAL SCRIPTURES

- Not every one that saith unto me, Lord, Lord, shall enter into the kingdom of heaven; but he that doeth the will of my Father which is in heaven. (Matthew 7:21)

- He that had been possessed with the devil prayed him that he might be with him. Howbeit Jesus suffered him not, but saith unto him, Go home to thy friends, and tell them how great things the Lord hath done for thee. (Mark 5:18–19)

- Ye call me Master and Lord: and ye say well; for so I am. (John 13:13)

- Thomas answered and said unto [Jesus], My LORD and my God. (John 20:28)

- The word which God sent unto the children of Israel, preaching peace by Jesus Christ: (he is Lord of all). (Acts 10:36)

- Wherefore God also hath highly exalted him, and given him a name which is above every name: That at the name of Jesus every knee should bow, of things in heaven, and things in earth, and things under the earth; And that every tongue should confess that Jesus Christ is Lord, to the glory of God the Father. (Philippians 2:9–11)

- And [Jesus] hath on his vesture and on his thigh a name written, KING OF KINGS, AND LORD OF LORDS. (Revelation 19:16)

WHAT OTHERS SAY

There is coming a day when every person who has ever lived will bow and acknowledge that Jesus Christ is King of Kings and Lord of Lords. But for the Christian that great confession should be an everyday reality. *Roger Willmore*

SO WHAT?

"If thou shalt confess with thy mouth the Lord Jesus, and shalt believe in thine heart that God hath raised him from the dead, thou shalt be saved." (Romans 10:9)

MAN OF SORROWS

IN TEN WORDS OR LESS
Jesus carried the full weight of this world's sin.

DETAILS, PLEASE
This phrase is found only once in the Bible, in a prophecy of Isaiah: "He is despised and rejected of men; a man of sorrows, and acquainted with grief: and we hid as it were our faces from him; he was despised, and we esteemed him not" (Isaiah 53:3). Jesus is often pictured as a "man of sorrows": weeping over the death of His friend, Lazarus (John 11:35); saddened by the hardness of human hearts (Mark 3:5); grieving the unbelief of Jerusalem (Matthew 23:37); experiencing the betrayal of close friends (Luke 22:48, Matthew 26:75). But the greatest sorrow—beyond the comprehension of our human minds—was Jesus' separation from His own Father, as the sins of all people were placed on Him on the cross.

ADDITIONAL SCRIPTURES
- And about the ninth hour Jesus cried with a loud voice, saying, Eli, Eli, lama sabachthani? that is to say, My God, my God, why hast thou forsaken me? (Matthew 27:46)

- And at the ninth hour Jesus cried with a loud voice, saying, Eloi, Eloi, lama sabachthani? which is, being interpreted, My God, my God, why hast thou forsaken me? (Mark 15:34)

WHAT OTHERS SAY
Is not the title, "man of sorrows," given to our Lord by way of eminence? He was not only sorrowful, but preeminent among the sorrowful. All men have a burden to bear, but His was heaviest of all. *Charles H. Spurgeon*

SO WHAT?
When life becomes hard—and it will for everyone, at some point—we know that Jesus understands our pain.

Master

In Ten Words or Less

Jesus is the boss—both of people and nature.

Details, Please

When you see Jesus called *master* in the King James Version, newer translations often say "teacher." But sometimes, *master* implies a commander more than an instructor—such as when the disciples, caught in a fierce storm on the Sea of Galilee, begged Jesus for help: "They came to him, and awoke him, saying, Master, master, we perish. Then he arose, and rebuked the wind and the raging of the water: and they ceased, and there was a calm" (Luke 8:24).

Additional Scriptures

- [Jesus] said unto Simon, Launch out into the deep, and let down your nets for a draught. And Simon answering said unto him, Master, we have toiled all the night, and have taken nothing: nevertheless at thy word I will let down the net. And when they had this done, they inclosed a great multitude of fishes: and their net brake. (Luke 5:4–6)

- Peter said unto Jesus, Master, it is good for us to be here: and let us make three tabernacles; one for thee, and one for Moses, and one for Elias: not knowing what he said. While he thus spake, there came a cloud, and overshadowed them: and they feared as they entered into the cloud. And there came a voice out of the cloud, saying, This is my beloved Son: hear him. (Luke 9:33–35)

What Others Say

Those that in sincerity call Christ *Master*, and with faith and fervency call upon him as *their Master*, may be sure that He will not let them perish. *Matthew Henry*

So What?

You are not the boss—Jesus is. Accept that fact, and dispense with a lot of stress in your life.

MEDIATOR

IN TEN WORDS OR LESS
Jesus is the perfect peacemaker between God and humanity.

DETAILS, PLEASE

Human sin offends God and separates every individual from Him. People need help to approach a perfect God, and that help is Jesus, the "one mediator between God and men" (1 Timothy 2:5). Since Jesus is both God and human, He could bridge the otherwise impassible gap between the two parties. Jesus' death on the cross satisfied God's demand that sin be punished; when we simply believe on this work, Jesus brings us and God into a relationship of peace and love.

ADDITIONAL SCRIPTURES

- But now hath [Jesus] obtained a more excellent ministry, by how much also he is the mediator of a better covenant, which was established upon better promises. (Hebrews 8:6)

- And for this cause [Jesus] is the mediator of the new testament, that by means of death, for the redemption of the transgressions that were under the first testament, they which are called might receive the promise of eternal inheritance. (Hebrews 9:15)

- But ye are come unto. . .Jesus the mediator of the new covenant. (Hebrews 12:22, 24)

WHAT OTHERS SAY

Come to Jesus directly, even to Jesus Himself. You do want a mediator between yourselves and God, but you do not want a mediator between yourselves and Jesus. Christ Jesus is the Mediator between you and the Father; but you need no one to stand between you and Christ. *Charles H. Spurgeon*

SO WHAT?

We simply can't please God on our own, so why try? Believing in Jesus opens the door to an everlasting and perfect relationship (John 14:6).

MESSIAH

IN TEN WORDS OR LESS
Jesus is the "chosen one" sent to save the world.

DETAILS, PLEASE
Are you surprised to learn that the term *Messiah* appears only four times in the King James Version? (Modern translations use it more often: the New International Version contains sixty-five instances, and the New Living Translation eighty-four.) *Messiah* is a Hebrew term translated into Greek as *Christ*; both of the King James Version's New Testament references appear in John: "We have found the Messias, which is, being interpreted, the Christ" (1:41); "The woman saith unto him, I know that Messias cometh, which is called Christ" (4:25). Meaning "the anointed one," the terms indicate the Person God specially set apart to save the world. Jesus said of Himself, "The Spirit of the Lord is upon me, because he hath anointed me to preach the gospel to the poor; he hath sent me to heal the brokenhearted, to preach deliverance to the captives, and recovering of sight to the blind, to set at liberty them that are bruised, to preach the acceptable year of the Lord" (Luke 4:18–19).

ADDITIONAL SCRIPTURES
• Know therefore and understand, that from the going forth of the commandment to restore and to build Jerusalem unto the Messiah the Prince shall be seven weeks, and threescore and two weeks. . . . And after threescore and two weeks shall Messiah be cut off, but not for himself. (Daniel 9:25–26)

WHAT OTHERS SAY
When we say Jesus Christ, we should be thinking in our mind Jesus the Messiah; Jesus the promised Priest, King, Prophet; Jesus the one who is anointed by God to bring about our redemption.
D. A. Carson

SO WHAT?
God the Father had a plan to save sinful humanity—Jesus was chosen so that you could be chosen too.

Miracle Worker

In Ten Words or Less

Jesus can overrule natural laws, because He created them.

Details, Please

Though all four Gospel writers depict Jesus performing miracles—healing illnesses, exorcising demons, overruling the laws of nature—John placed a heavy emphasis on the word, often translated "signs" in more modern translations. It was John who identified Jesus' first miracle, the changing of water into wine at a wedding celebration: "This beginning of miracles did Jesus in Cana of Galilee, and manifested forth his glory; and his disciples believed on him" (2:11). Soon afterward, Jesus was attracting additional followers by His unusual powers: "Now when he was in Jerusalem at the passover, in the feast day, many believed in his name, when they saw the miracles which he did" (2:23). In time, "a great multitude" surrounded Jesus because of His willingness and ability to heal people (6:1–2). Even His enemies admitted that Jesus' powers were remarkable—and a threat to their own position: "Then gathered the chief priests and the Pharisees a council, and said, What do we? for this man doeth many miracles. If we let him thus alone, all men will believe on him: and the Romans shall come and take away both our place and nation" (11:47–48).

John's emphasis on Jesus' miraculous powers supports his book's prologue, which identifies Jesus as God and the creator of all things (1:1–3). Ultimately, John's point is that Jesus not only protects and heals bodies, but souls: "And many other signs truly did Jesus in the presence of his disciples, which are not written in this book: But these are written, that ye might believe that Jesus is the Christ, the Son of God; and that believing ye might have life through his name" (20:30–31).

Additional Scriptures

- When [the disciples] saw [Jesus] walking upon the sea, they supposed it had been a spirit, and cried out: For they all saw him, and were troubled. And immediately he talked with them, and saith unto them, Be of good cheer: it is I; be not afraid. And he went up unto them into the ship; and the wind ceased: and they were sore amazed in themselves beyond measure, and wondered. For they considered not the miracle of the loaves: for their heart was hardened. (Mark 6:49–52)

- And when Herod saw Jesus, he was exceeding glad: for he was desirous to see him of a long season, because he had heard many things of him; and he hoped to have seen some miracle done by him. (Luke 23:8)

- Ye men of Israel, hear these words; Jesus of Nazareth, a man approved of God among you by miracles and wonders and signs, which God did by him in the midst of you, as ye yourselves also know. (Acts 2:22)

WHAT OTHERS SAY

If we are to understand who Jesus is, we must understand the significance of His miracles. One thing they were not: a means for Jesus to show off or gain anything for Himself. Not once does the Bible—or any other source—suggest that Jesus used His miracles to advance Himself or His followers. Rather, Jesus doggedly stuck to the role of humble servant. *Sheri Bell*

SO WHAT?

Whatever need you have—physical, emotional, financial, spiritual—is well within the power of the all-knowing, all-powerful, loving and generous Jesus.

NAZARENE

IN TEN WORDS OR LESS
Jesus would be identified by His humble, disrespected hometown.

DETAILS, PLEASE
Matthew's Gospel says that Mary's husband, Joseph, settled his new family in the town of Nazareth, in fulfillment of a prophecy that Jesus would be "called a Nazarene" (2:23). But the town is not mentioned anywhere in the Old Testament. Bible scholars suggest a few solutions to the mystery: perhaps this prophecy came down through oral tradition; *Nazarene* may be a rendering of the Hebrew word for "branch" in the prophecy of Isaiah 11:1; or the name might simply indicate a person held in low esteem. Jesus' disciple Nathanael originally scoffed at the idea of the Messiah coming from that particular town: "Can there any good thing come out of Nazareth?" (John 1:46).

ADDITIONAL SCRIPTURES
- And [Mary's husband, Joseph] came and dwelt in a city called Nazareth: that it might be fulfilled which was spoken by the prophets, He [Jesus] shall be called a Nazarene. (Matthew 2:23)

- We have found this man [Paul] a pestilent fellow, and a mover of sedition among all the Jews throughout the world, and a ringleader of the sect of the Nazarenes. (Acts 24:5)

WHAT OTHERS SAY
Hereby was fulfilled what has been spoken in effect by several of the prophets (though by none of them in express words) He shall be called a Nazarene—that is, He shall be despised and rejected, shall be a mark of public contempt and reproach. *John Wesley*

SO WHAT?
If you've ever been looked down on, Jesus knows just how you feel.

Peace

Jesus removes humanity's greatest conflict—enmity with God.

Details, Please
While numerous passages relate Jesus to peace, one specifically *calls* Him "peace": "But now in Christ Jesus ye who sometimes were far off are made nigh by the blood of Christ. For he is our peace, who hath made both [Jew and Gentile] one, and hath broken down the middle wall of partition between us; having abolished in his flesh the enmity, even the law of commandments contained in ordinances; for to make in himself of twain one new man, so making peace" (Ephesians 2:13–15). This statement from the apostle Paul is the logical outgrowth of a familiar prophecy of Isaiah: "For unto us a child is born, unto us a son is given: and the government shall be upon his shoulder: and his name shall be called Wonderful, Counsellor, The mighty God, The everlasting Father, The Prince of Peace" (Isaiah 9:6).

Additional Scriptures
- Peace I leave with you, my peace I give unto you: not as the world giveth, give I unto you. Let not your heart be troubled, neither let it be afraid. (John 14:27)

- These things I have spoken unto you, that in me ye might have peace. In the world ye shall have tribulation: but be of good cheer; I have overcome the world. (John 16:33)

- Then said Jesus to them again, Peace be unto you: as my Father hath sent me, even so send I you. (John 20:21)

- The word which God sent unto the children of Israel, preaching peace by Jesus Christ: (he is Lord of all). (Acts 10:36)

- Therefore being justified by faith, we have peace with God through our Lord Jesus Christ. (Romans 5:1)

- For it pleased the Father that in him should all fulness dwell; and, having made peace through the blood of his cross, by him to reconcile all things unto himself; by him,

I say, whether they be things in earth, or things in heaven. (Colossians 1:19–20)

- Grace be unto you, and peace, from God our Father, and from the Lord Jesus Christ. (1 Corinthians 1:3; see very similar comments in 2 Corinthians 1:2; Galatians 1:3; Ephesians 1:2; Philippians 1:2, 1 Thessalonians 1:1; 2 Thessalonians 1:2; 1 Timothy 1:2; 2 Timothy 1:2; Titus 1:4; Philemon 3; 1 Peter 1:2; 2 Peter 1:2; 2 John 1:3)

WHAT OTHERS SAY

God is a peace-loving God, and a peacemaking God. The whole history of redemption, climaxing in the death and resurrection of Jesus, is God's strategy to bring about a just and lasting peace between rebel man and Himself, and then between man and his fellow man. *John Piper*

SO WHAT?

Few of us enjoy conflict. Through Jesus, our single most troubling conflict—our ongoing human battle against God—can be completely eliminated. And then we can begin to deal with our conflicts with others.

PROPHET

Jesus foretold the future and "forthtold" God's message to people.

DETAILS, PLEASE

Biblical prophets had two main jobs (telling the future and sharing God's message to the people around them) and often a common characteristic (the working of miracles). Jesus checked the box on all three. He predicted His own death and resurrection (Mark 8:31) as well as the destruction of Jerusalem and/or the end of time (Matthew 24–25). Though Jesus is God, as the Son He carried the Father's message to the world: "as my Father hath taught me, I speak these things" (John 8:28). His miracles are well known, from the raising of Lazarus from the dead to feeding five thousand men with fives loaves of bread and two fish. The latter caused people to say, "This is of a truth that prophet that should come into the world" (John 6:14). Jesus applied the title *prophet* to Himself on occasion, such as when He criticized His hometown of Nazareth for its unbelief: "Verily I say unto you, No prophet is accepted in his own country" (Luke 4:24).

ADDITIONAL SCRIPTURE

- And when he was come into Jerusalem, all the city was moved, saying, Who is this? And the multitude said, This is Jesus the prophet of Nazareth of Galilee. (Matthew 21:10–11)

- And when the chief priests and Pharisees had heard his parables, they perceived that he spake of them. But when they sought to lay hands on him, they feared the multitude, because they took him for a prophet. (Matthew 21:45–46)

- And it came to pass, as he was alone praying, his disciples were with him: and he asked them, saying, Whom say the people that I am? They answering said, John the Baptist; but some say, Elias; and others say, that one of the old prophets is risen again. (Luke 9:18–19)

- Nevertheless I must walk to day, and to morrow, and the day following: for it cannot be that a prophet perish out of Jerusalem. (Luke 13:33)

- And he said unto them, What things? And they said unto him, Concerning Jesus of Nazareth, which was a prophet mighty in deed and word before God and all the people. (Luke 24:19)

- The woman saith unto him, Sir, I perceive that thou art a prophet. (John 4:19)

- Many of the people therefore, when they heard this saying, said, Of a truth this is the Prophet. (John 7:40)

- They say unto the blind man again, What sayest thou of him, that he hath opened thine eyes? He said, He is a prophet. (John 9:17)

WHAT OTHERS SAY
Jesus Christ is the Prophet of Christendom. His words must always be the first and the last appeal. *Charles H. Spurgeon*

SO WHAT?
Prophets carry God's message to us. We should pay careful attention to what they say—especially when that prophet is Jesus.

REDEEMER

IN TEN WORDS OR LESS

Jesus "buys back" people who were trapped in their sin.

DETAILS, PLEASE

In the King James Version, the word *redeemer* appears only in the Old Testament, often in connection with God the Father—though a comment from the ancient sufferer Job is thought to be a very early hint of Jesus: "I know that my redeemer liveth, and that he shall stand at the latter day upon the earth" (Job 19:25). A redeemer is one who buys something back or frees from captivity, ideas that certainly apply to the work of Jesus in winning people back from their bondage to sin. As the apostle Paul wrote, "Christ hath redeemed us from the curse of the law, being made a curse for us: for it is written, Cursed is every one that hangeth on a tree" (Galatians 3:13). And Peter added to that thought by saying, "Ye know that ye were not redeemed with corruptible things, as silver and gold, from your vain conversation received by tradition from your fathers; but with the precious blood of Christ, as of a lamb without blemish and without spot" (1 Peter 1:18–19).

ADDITIONAL SCRIPTURES

- Being justified freely by his grace through the redemption that is in Christ Jesus: Whom God hath set forth to be a propitiation through faith in his blood, to declare his righteousness for the remission of sins that are past. (Romans 3:24–25)

- But when the fulness of the time was come, God sent forth his Son, made of a woman, made under the law, to redeem them that were under the law, that we might receive the adoption of sons. (Galatians 4:4–5)

- Having predestinated us unto the adoption of children by Jesus Christ to himself, according to the good pleasure of his will, to the praise of the glory of his grace, wherein he hath made us accepted in the beloved. In whom we have redemption through his blood, the forgiveness of sins, according to the riches of his grace. (Ephesians 1:5–7)

- [God] hath delivered us from the power of darkness, and hath translated us into the kingdom of his dear Son: In whom we have redemption through his blood, even the forgiveness of sins. (Colossians 1:13–14)

- And they sung a new song, saying, Thou [Jesus] art worthy to take the book, and to open the seals thereof: for thou wast slain, and hast redeemed us to God by thy blood out of every kindred, and tongue, and people, and nation. (Revelation 5:9)

WHAT OTHERS SAY

My sins were all upon Him laid,
A full atonement He hath made,
For me He hath the ransom paid;
Christ is my Redeemer.
Daniel W. Whittle

SO WHAT?

Redemption is not an accidental thing—Jesus consciously and intentionally gave His life to purchase your freedom. Have you accepted the gift He offers?

Resurrection and the Life

In Ten Words or Less
Since Jesus defeated death, He'll help us defeat death too.

Details, Please
Though every person is literally born dying, human nature is to extend life as long as possible, to fight against those forces—human or otherwise—that would take life. Though death is inevitable, we simply don't want to die. . .that's why this name for Jesus is so appealing.

After His friend Lazarus took ill and died, Jesus visited the man's grieving sisters, telling Martha, "I am the resurrection, and the life: he that believeth in me, though he were dead, yet shall he live: and whosoever liveth and believeth in me shall never die" (John 11:25–26). Then, seemingly to confirm the truth of His statement, Jesus brought Lazarus back to life, four days after his passing.

Lazarus was one of a handful of dead people that Jesus raised to life during His time on earth. But a day will come when He'll give everlasting life to everyone who has chosen to follow Him. As Jesus told the Jewish leaders who opposed Him, "the hour is coming, in the which all that are in the graves shall hear his [Jesus'] voice, and shall come forth; they that have done good, unto the resurrection of life; and they that have done evil, unto the resurrection of damnation" (John 5:28–29).

Additional Scriptures
- And the graves were opened; and many bodies of the saints which slept arose, and came out of the graves after his resurrection, and went into the holy city, and appeared unto many (Matthew 27:52–53).

- And some said, What will this babbler [Paul] say? other some, He seemeth to be a setter forth of strange gods: because he preached unto them Jesus, and the resurrection. (Acts 17:18)

- And declared to be the Son of God with power, according to the spirit of holiness, by the resurrection from the dead. (Romans 1:4)

- For if we have been planted together in the likeness of his death, we shall be also in the likeness of his resurrection. (Romans 6:5)

- For since by man came death, by man came also the resurrection of the dead. (1 Corinthians 15:21)

- Blessed be the God and Father of our Lord Jesus Christ, which according to his abundant mercy hath begotten us again unto a lively hope by the resurrection of Jesus Christ from the dead. (1 Peter 1:3)

WHAT OTHERS SAY

They who believe in Christ, though they were formerly dead, begin to live, because faith is a spiritual resurrection of the soul, and—so to speak—animates the soul itself that it may live to God. *John Calvin*

SO WHAT?

Death is always an enemy (1 Corinthians 15:26), but it is not invincible. We don't need to fear death since Jesus is the resurrection and the life.

Rider on a White Horse

In Ten Words or Less
Jesus will someday return to earth as a conquering king.

Details, Please
On His last journey to Jerusalem, to fulfill Zechariah's prophecy (9:9), Jesus rode into the city "meek, and sitting upon an ass, and a colt the foal of an ass" (Matthew 21:5). But a day is coming when He will be anything but meek, returning to earth on a white warhorse, bent on conquest (see below).

Additional Scripture
- And I saw heaven opened, and behold a white horse; and he that sat upon him was called Faithful and True, and in righteousness he doth judge and make war. His eyes were as a flame of fire, and on his head were many crowns; and he had a name written, that no man knew, but he himself. And he was clothed with a vesture dipped in blood: and his name is called The Word of God. And the armies which were in heaven followed him upon white horses, clothed in fine linen, white and clean. And out of his mouth goeth a sharp sword, that with it he should smite the nations: and he shall rule them with a rod of iron: and he treadeth the winepress of the fierceness and wrath of Almighty God. And he hath on his vesture and on his thigh a name written, King Of Kings, And Lord Of Lords. (Revelation 19:11–16)

What Others Say
In the day of His humiliation he rode but once—when He came to the Jewish nation as its anointed king. But He then rode upon an ass, a colt, the foal of an ass. Then He was the meek and lowly one; but here the little domestic animal is exchanged for the martial charger, for this is another and mightier coming as the King of the World. *Joseph Seiss*

So What?
Jesus was once humbled so that He (and we, with Him) would ultimately be honored.

Risen Lord

In Ten Words or Less
Jesus promised to rise from the dead—and He did.

Details, Please
This name for Jesus is not an exact Bible quote, but a synthesis of several passages. After His death on the cross, Jesus spent parts of three days in a tomb before returning to life and visiting His disciples. The words of an angel at the empty grave encapsulate this title: "He is not here: for he is risen, as he said. Come, see the place where the Lord lay" (Matthew 28:6). Later that day, Jesus' disciples used a phrase that became an Easter greeting for many Christians: "The Lord is risen indeed" (Luke 24:34)

Additional Scriptures
- And as they came down from the mountain, Jesus charged them, saying, Tell the vision to no man, until the Son of man be risen again from the dead. (Matthew 17:9)

- Who is he that condemneth? It is Christ that died, yea rather, that is risen again, who is even at the right hand of God, who also maketh intercession for us. (Romans 8:34)

- But if there be no resurrection of the dead, then is Christ not risen: And if Christ be not risen, then is our preaching vain, and your faith is also vain. . . . But now is Christ risen from the dead, and become the firstfruits of them that slept. (1 Corinthians 15:13–14, 20)

What Others Say
If the bones of Jesus lie decayed in a grave, then there is no Good News, and the world is still in darkness. Life has no meaning at all. The New Testament then becomes a myth and Christianity is a fable. . . . However, the New Testament teaches that Christ is indeed risen from the dead. The greatest and most thrilling fact of human history is the resurrection of Jesus Christ. *Billy Graham*

So What?
By overcoming His own death, Jesus showed a power that allows Him to overcome our death, as well.

SACRIFICE

IN TEN WORDS OR LESS
Jesus was the offering that permanently removes human sin.

DETAILS, PLEASE
The book of Hebrews speaks at length of the sacrifice Jesus made for sin. By offering Himself on the cross as payment for every person's disobedience toward God, Jesus made a way for humans to be "saved" from the punishment of hell. (See Hebrews 5–10 for details.) But it was the apostle Paul who actually described Jesus as a "sacrifice," when he wrote to the church in Ephesus, "Walk in love, as Christ also hath loved us, and hath given himself for us an offering and a sacrifice to God for a sweetsmelling savour" (Ephesians 5:2). Justice demanded that sin be punished, and God the Father generously accepted the willing sacrifice of Jesus, the Son: "Therefore doth my Father love me, because I lay down my life, that I might take it again. No man taketh it from me, but I lay it down of myself" (John 10:17–18).

ADDITIONAL SCRIPTURES
- For then must he often have suffered since the foundation of the world: but now once in the end of the world hath he appeared to put away sin by the sacrifice of himself. (Hebrews 9:26)

WHAT OTHERS SAY
Christ's sacrifice is perpetually effective. It is unique. It does not recur. It cannot be copied or imitated. But the Lord's Table points back to it, and our own sufferings are to be aligned with it as we, in turn, ourselves, may commend the cross of Christ to others today. *D. A. Carson*

SO WHAT?
Don't worry about "making things right" with God—Jesus has already done that for you. Just believe and enjoy the results.

Same Yesterday, Today, and Forever

In Ten Words or Less
Since Jesus is perfect, He does not change.

Details, Please
At the end of the book of Hebrews are several "exhortations"—encouragements to do the right thing. Amidst calls to love one another, show hospitality, be content, and honor church leaders is a reminder that "Jesus Christ [is] the same yesterday, and to day, and for ever" (13:8). Since He is God, Jesus is perfect, and He has no need or inclination to change. This "immutability" gives us confidence in our relationship to Him, and a powerful reason to do what He tells us to do.

Additional Scripture
- For I am the LORD, I change not; therefore ye sons of Jacob are not consumed. (Malachi 3:6)

What Others Say
If he were fickle, vacillating, changing in His character and plans; if today He aids His people, and tomorrow will forsake them; if at one time He loves the virtuous, and at another equally loves the vicious; if He formed a plan yesterday which He has abandoned today; or if He is ever to be a different being from what He is now, there would be no encouragement to effort. Who would know what to depend on? Who would know what to expect tomorrow? For who could have any certainty that he could ever please a capricious or a vacillating being? *Albert Barnes*

So What?
You can know Jesus through the Bible, and you can trust that He will not change—even when the world around you changes by the minute.

Savior

Jesus is the one who rescues people from their sin.

Details, Please

This name means "deliverer," and the Old Testament describes several people by that term. But their "saving" was limited in time and scope. Jesus' name and work excelled them all, as stated by an angel in the lead-up to the first Christmas: "The angel of the LORD appeared unto him in a dream, saying, Joseph, thou son of David, fear not to take unto thee Mary thy wife: for that which is conceived in her is of the Holy Ghost. And she shall bring forth a son, and thou shalt call his name JESUS: for he shall save his people from their sins" (Matthew 1:20–21). The name *Jesus* is derived from *Joshua*, an Old Testament name meaning "Jehovah is salvation," and identifies the baby born in Bethlehem with the eternal creator God. The disciple Peter also emphasized the deity of Jesus by writing, "Grow in grace, and in the knowledge of our Lord and Saviour Jesus Christ" (2 Peter 3:18).

Additional Scriptures

- For unto you is born this day in the city of David a Saviour, which is Christ the Lord. (Luke 2:11)

- And said unto the woman, Now we believe, not because of thy saying: for we have heard him ourselves, and know that this is indeed the Christ, the Saviour of the world. (John 4:42)

- Of this man's seed hath God according to his promise raised unto Israel a Saviour, Jesus. (Acts 13:23)

- For our conversation is in heaven; from whence also we look for the Saviour, the Lord Jesus Christ. (Philippians 3:20)

- Who hath saved us, and called us with an holy calling, not according to our works, but according to his own purpose and grace, which was given us in Christ Jesus before the world began, but is now made manifest by the appearing of our Saviour Jesus Christ, who hath abolished death, and hath brought life and immortality to light through the gospel. (2 Timothy 1:9–10)

- Looking for that blessed hope, and the glorious appearing of the great God and our Saviour Jesus Christ. (Titus 2:13)

- Not by works of righteousness which we have done, but according to his mercy he saved us, by the washing of regeneration, and renewing of the Holy Ghost; which he shed on us abundantly through Jesus Christ our Saviour. (Titus 3:5–6)

- And we have seen and do testify that the Father sent the Son to be the Saviour of the world. (1 John 4:14)

What Others Say

Joshua of old was a savior. Gideon was a savior. David was a savior. But the title is given to our Lord above all others because He is a Savior in a sense that no one else can be—He saves His people from their sins! *Charles H. Spurgeon*

So What?

Every one of us is born into this world lost and dying. Every one of us can be saved by Jesus, if only we'll ask.

SECOND PERSON OF THE TRINITY

IN TEN WORDS OR LESS
Jesus is God, yet distinct from the Father and Spirit.

DETAILS, PLEASE
The Bible presents one God in three persons—Father, Son, Holy Spirit—a concept theologians call the *trinity*, though that term is not used in scripture. A hint of the idea appears in the Bible's first chapter, when God says, "Let *us* make man in *our* image" (Genesis 1:26, emphasis added), and the Old Testament goes on to provide many prophecies of a coming Son who would serve, suffer, and save. After Jesus' birth, several New Testament passages mention all three members of the Trinity, including this one: "And Jesus, when he was baptized, went up straightway out of the water: and, lo, the heavens were opened unto him, and he saw the Spirit of God descending like a dove, and lighting upon him: And lo a voice from heaven, saying, This is my beloved Son, in whom I am well pleased" (Matthew 3:16–17).

ADDITIONAL SCRIPTURES
- Go ye therefore, and teach all nations, baptizing them in the name of the Father, and of the Son, and of the Holy Ghost. (Matthew 28:19)

- The grace of the Lord Jesus Christ, and the love of God, and the communion of the Holy Ghost, be with you all. Amen. (2 Corinthians 13:14)

- And because ye are sons, God hath sent forth the Spirit of his Son into your hearts, crying, Abba, Father. (Galatians 4:6)

WHAT OTHERS SAY
Monotheism was enriched, deepened by the revelation which God had given in Christ and at Pentecost. God was one, but He was not single; He was a complex, mysterious one, a unity of Father, Son, and Holy Spirit. *Fisher Humphries and Philip Wise*

SO WHAT?
The second person of the Trinity became a man, to be an example for us—and to suffer our punishment for sin.

SON OF DAVID

IN TEN WORDS OR LESS
Jesus is the fulfillment of God's promises to King David.

DETAILS, PLEASE
After David became king of Israel, his military successes brought peace to the land. He wanted to build a permanent home for the ark of the covenant, but God said no—however, He did promise David an ongoing kingdom, one that "shall be established for ever" (2 Samuel 7:16). Though David's nation would disintegrate and disappear in centuries to come, the birth of Jesus kept God's promise alive. As a direct descendant or "son" of David (see Matthew 1:1–17; Luke 3:23–38), Jesus will sit on an everlasting throne in the new heaven and new earth described in Revelation 21–22.

ADDITIONAL SCRIPTURES
- The book of the generation of Jesus Christ, the son of David, the son of Abraham. (Matthew 1:1).

- While the Pharisees were gathered together, Jesus asked them, saying, What think ye of Christ? whose son is he? They say unto him, The son of David. He saith unto them, How then doth David in spirit call him Lord, saying, The LORD said unto my Lord, Sit thou on my right hand, till I make thine enemies thy footstool? If David then call him Lord, how is he his son? And no man was able to answer him a word. (Matthew 22:41–46)

WHAT OTHERS SAY
Who is Jesus Christ? Who is this One, the God-Man? A Man, yes, a son of David but also David's Lord and the One who is forever seated as the power of God on the very throne of God, God Himself. *John MacArthur*

SO WHAT?
The "Son of David" is proof that God keeps His promises. You can trust Him completely.

Son of God

Within the triune Godhead, Jesus holds the position of Son.

Details, Please

This name was more often spoken *of* than *by* Jesus—though the apostle John does show Jesus using "Son of God" to describe Himself on a few occasions. In Luke's account of the annunciation (the announcement of Jesus' birth), the angel Gabriel told Mary that "that holy thing which shall be born of thee shall be called the Son of God" (Luke 1:35). Nathanael, who would become one of Jesus' twelve disciples, originally scoffed at the teacher from Nazareth, but quickly came to declare, "Rabbi, thou art the Son of God" (John 1:49). Even demons used the name, after Jesus cast them out of possessed individuals: "What have we to do with thee, Jesus, thou Son of God? art thou come hither to torment us before the time?" (Matthew 8:29). And the Roman centurion who witnessed Jesus' death on the cross said in wonder, "Truly this man was the Son of God" (Mark 15:39). For His part, Jesus applied the phrase to Himself in the third person: "He that believeth not is condemned already, because he hath not believed in the name of the only begotten Son of God" (John 3:18); "The hour is coming, and now is, when the dead shall hear the voice of the Son of God: and they that hear shall live" (John 5:25); "Dost thou believe on the Son of God?" (John 9:35); "This sickness is not unto death, but for the glory of God, that the Son of God might be glorified thereby" (John 11:4).

Additional Scriptures

- And when [the disciples] were come into the ship, the wind ceased. Then they that were in the ship came and worshipped him, saying, Of a truth thou art the Son of God. (Matthew 14:32–33)

- And the high priest answered and said unto him, I adjure thee by the living God, that thou tell us whether thou be the Christ, the Son of God. Jesus saith unto him, Thou hast said. (Matthew 26:63–64)

- The chief priests mocking him, with the scribes and elders, said. . .He trusted in God; let him deliver him now, if he will have him: for he said, I am the Son of God. (Matthew 27:41, 43)

- The beginning of the gospel of Jesus Christ, the Son of God. . . (Mark 1:1)

- And I saw, and bare record that this is the Son of God. (John 1:34)

- Seeing then that we have a great high priest, that is passed into the heavens, Jesus the Son of God, let us hold fast our profession. (Hebrews 4:14)

- Whosoever shall confess that Jesus is the Son of God, God dwelleth in him, and he in God. (1 John 4:15)

WHAT OTHERS SAY

Jesus is God's Son. He is the Promised One. Not *a* Son of God, as some of our learned critics condescendingly say, but *the* Son of God. We should seek to be like John the Baptist—a sign-post pointing to Him and saying, "Behold! the Son of God." *Charles Hurlburt and T. C. Horton*

SO WHAT?

If you want to please a good father, show honor to his son. If you want to please God the Father, honor Jesus Christ.

Son of Man

In Ten Words or Less
Jesus' preferred name for Himself indicates both humanity and deity.

Details, Please
Thirty times in the Gospel of Matthew, fourteen times in Mark, twenty-six times in Luke, and nine times in John, Jesus calls Himself "the Son of man." Though the phrase implies His humanness (God often called the Old Testament prophet Ezekiel "Son of man"), Jesus was probably applying another prophetic reference to Himself—this one from the book of Daniel: "I saw in the night visions, and, behold, one like the Son of man came with the clouds of heaven, and came to the Ancient of days, and they brought him near before him. And there was given him dominion, and glory, and a kingdom, that all people, nations, and languages, should serve him: his dominion is an everlasting dominion, which shall not pass away, and his kingdom that which shall not be destroyed" (7:13–14). Though Jesus did not often identify Himself as the Son of God or the Messiah, His calling Himself "Son of man" carried the same message to those familiar with Daniel's prophecy.

Additional Scriptures
- And Jesus saith unto him, The foxes have holes, and the birds of the air have nests; but the Son of man hath not where to lay his head. (Matthew 8:20)

- When Jesus came into the coasts of Caesarea Philippi, he asked his disciples, saying, Whom do men say that I the Son of man am? (Matthew 16:13)

- And as they came down from the mountain, Jesus charged them, saying, Tell the vision to no man, until the Son of man be risen again from the dead. (Matthew 17:9)

- And Jesus said, I am: and ye shall see the Son of man sitting on the right hand of power, and coming in the clouds of heaven. (Mark 14:62)

- But Jesus said unto him, Judas, betrayest thou the Son of man with a kiss? (Luke 22:48)

- Saying, The Son of man must be delivered into the hands of sinful men, and be crucified, and the third day rise again. (Luke 24:7)

- Then said Jesus unto them, When ye have lifted up the Son of man, then shall ye know that I am he, and that I do nothing of myself; but as my Father hath taught me, I speak these things. (John 8:28)

- And Jesus answered them, saying, The hour is come, that the Son of man should be glorified. (John 12:23)

WHAT OTHERS SAY

"Son of Man" has the double meaning of human being and, according to Daniel 7, exalted heavenly one. And Jesus means to communicate both of those. *John Piper*

SO WHAT?

Since He's fully human, Jesus understands the challenges, stresses, and temptations of His people. Since He's fully God, He has the power to help us overcome.

STAR

IN TEN WORDS OR LESS
As stars do physically, Jesus provides light and warmth spiritually.

DETAILS, PLEASE
On several occasions, the Bible likens Jesus to a star. He described Himself as "the bright and morning star" in Revelation 22:16. This likely indicates the dawning of a new day—the perfection of eternity—by referencing the planet Venus, which glows like a star as the sun rises. The apostle Peter made a similar reference, calling Jesus the "day star" that rises in believers' hearts (2 Peter 1:19). And there are at least two prophetic references in the Old Testament that identify the coming Messiah as a star (see below).

ADDITIONAL SCRIPTURES
- I shall see him, but not now: I shall behold him, but not nigh: there shall come a Star out of Jacob, and a Sceptre shall rise out of Israel, and shall smite the corners of Moab, and destroy all the children of Sheth. (Numbers 24:17)

- For, behold, the day cometh, that shall burn as an oven; and all the proud, yea, and all that do wickedly, shall be stubble: and the day that cometh shall burn them up, saith the LORD of hosts, that it shall leave them neither root nor branch. But unto you that fear my name shall the Sun of righteousness arise with healing in his wings. (Malachi 4:1–2)

WHAT OTHERS SAY
What better way to greet the dawning of each new day than to breathe a prayer of thanks to God for sending His Bright and Morning Star into the world? *George W. Knight*

SO WHAT?
If you're lost in the darkness, look up to Jesus. He's the star that guides you through.

STONE

Jesus is solid, strong, reliable—and dangerous to His enemies.

DETAILS, PLEASE

A stone is a common image for Jesus throughout the New Testament. The Lord Himself used it, referencing Psalm 118:22, as recorded by Matthew (21:42, 44), Mark (12:10–11), and Luke (20:17–18): "What is this then that is written, The stone which the builders rejected, the same is become the head of the corner? Whosoever shall fall upon that stone shall be broken; but on whomsoever it shall fall, it will grind him to powder." In a sermon preached in Jerusalem (Acts 4), the apostle Peter alluded to the same psalm, and later referenced Isaiah 28:16 when he wrote of Jesus as a "living stone, disallowed indeed of men, but chosen of God, and precious" (1 Peter 2:4). The apostle Paul also identified Jesus as a stone or rock on several occasions (see below).

ADDITIONAL SCRIPTURES

- As it is written, Behold, I lay in Sion a stumblingstone and rock of offence: and whosoever believeth on him shall not be ashamed. (Romans 9:33)

- All our fathers were under the cloud, and all passed through the sea; And were all baptized unto Moses in the cloud and in the sea; And did all eat the same spiritual meat; And did all drink the same spiritual drink: for they drank of that spiritual Rock that followed them: and that Rock was Christ. (1 Corinthians 10:1–4)

- Now therefore ye are no more strangers and foreigners, but fellowcitizens with the saints, and of the household of God; And are built upon the foundation of the apostles and prophets, Jesus Christ himself being the chief corner stone; In whom all the building fitly framed together groweth unto an holy temple in the Lord. (Ephesians 2:19–21)

What Others Say

[Jesus] was a stone evidently of God's quarrying and preparing. His extraordinary birth marked Him out as differing from all the rest of mankind; His surpassing excellence and moral beauty declared Him to be destined to the highest position. His person displayed the marvellous love and wisdom of God. *Charles H. Spurgeon*

So What?

When your world seems shaky and troubled, you have a solid place to stand, a strong refuge where you can hide—Jesus, our Rock or Stone.

SUBSTITUTE

IN TEN WORDS OR LESS

In His death, Jesus took the punishment for our sins.

DETAILS, PLEASE

You won't find *substitute* as a name or title of Jesus in the King James Version of the Bible, nor in the New International, New Living, or English Standard translations. But the idea is certainly there, perhaps nowhere more clearly than in Romans 5:6–8: "For when we were yet without strength, in due time Christ died for the ungodly. For scarcely for a righteous man will one die: yet peradventure for a good man some would even dare to die. But God commendeth his love toward us, in that, while we were yet sinners, Christ died for us." Other passages support this idea of His substitutionary death (see below), but even an enemy of Jesus once inadvertently prophesied it. Caiaphas, the Jewish high priest in Jesus' day, hated Him and wanted to see Him dead. "It is expedient for us," Caiaphas told the chief priests and Pharisees, "that one man should die for the people, and that the whole nation perish not" (John 11:50). The apostle John's perspective? "This spake he not of himself: but being high priest that year, he prophesied that Jesus should die for that nation; and not for that nation only, but that also he should gather together in one the children of God that were scattered abroad" (John 11:51–52).

ADDITIONAL SCRIPTURES

- The next day John seeth Jesus coming unto him, and saith, Behold the Lamb of God, which taketh away the sin of the world. (John 1:29)

- I am the good shepherd: the good shepherd giveth his life for the sheep. (John 10:11)

- For he hath made him to be sin for us, who knew no sin; that we might be made the righteousness of God in him. (2 Corinthians 5:21)

- And that he died for all, that they which live should not henceforth live unto themselves, but unto him which died for them, and rose again. (2 Corinthians 5:15)

- Christ hath redeemed us from the curse of the law, being made a curse for us: for it is written, Cursed is every one that hangeth on a tree. (Galatians 3:13)

- [Jesus], who his own self bare our sins in his own body on the tree, that we, being dead to sins, should live unto righteousness: by whose stripes ye were healed. (1 Peter 2:24)

WHAT OTHERS SAY

We are acceptable to God not because we have obeyed, nor because we have promised to give up things, but because of the death of Christ, and for no other reason. *Oswald Chambers*

SO WHAT?

The beauty of Christianity is that we never have to be "good enough" for God. *Jesus* was good enough—and all we need to do is believe and receive His salvation.

Sustainer of All Things

In Ten Words or Less

Jesus not only made the world, He holds it together.

Details, Please

We've already seen Jesus' role as Creator of all things (page 21), but He is even more than that. Jesus is the force that keeps the entire universe in operation. As the writer of Hebrews put it, Jesus is "upholding all things by the word of his power" (1:3), or, in the language of the New International Version, "sustaining all things by his powerful word." The original Greek verb indicates that Jesus "carries" all things—it's the same word that Peter used to describe how Bible writers were "carried along" (NIV) by the Holy Spirit to write exactly what God wanted them to. With God, nothing is left to chance.

Additional Scriptures

- For by [Jesus] were all things created, that are in heaven, and that are in earth, visible and invisible, whether they be thrones, or dominions, or principalities, or powers: all things were created by him, and for him: and he is before all things, and by him all things consist. (Colossians 1:16–17)

- But to us there is but one God, the Father, of whom are all things, and we in him; and one Lord Jesus Christ, by whom are all things, and we by him [*through whom we live*, NIV, NLT]. (1 Corinthians 8:6)

What Others Say

This is an astonishing description of the infinitely energetic and all-pervading power of God. He spake, and all things were created; He speaks, and all things are sustained. *Adam Clarke*

So What?

No matter how chaotic the world (or, more specifically, your own life) may seem, Jesus is there, holding everything together. Nothing is beyond His knowledge or His controlling power.

Teacher (Rabbi)

In Ten Words or Less
Jesus not only saves but teaches us how to live.

Details, Please
When Jesus called Peter, Andrew, James, and John to leave their fishing nets and "follow" Him (Matthew 4:18–22), He was inviting them to learn from His teaching, to "conform wholly to His example," according to Thayer's Greek-English Lexicon. The prominent Pharisee Nicodemus, the first person to hear the words we now know as John 3:16, identified Jesus' role as teacher when he began his nighttime visit with the Lord in Jerusalem: "Rabbi, we know that thou art a teacher come from God: for no man can do these miracles that thou doest, except God be with him" (John 3:2).

Additional Scriptures
- Turning around, Jesus saw them following and asked, "What do you want?" They said, "Rabbi" (which means "Teacher"), "where are you staying?" (John 1:38 NIV)

- "You call me 'Teacher' and 'Lord,' and rightly so, for that is what I am." (John 13:13 NIV)

- But be not ye called Rabbi: for one is your Master, even Christ; and all ye are brethren. (Matthew 23:8)

What Others Say
The disciples recognize in [Jesus] their teacher and master. They should, therefore, follow His example by helping each other even in the lowliest services. The Master had set an example which the slave need not be ashamed to copy. If they realize that by doing such things He has made it their duty to do the same, then they will be happy in the doing of them. *Arthur Peake*

So What?
We all need guidance, both for this life and the life to come—and Jesus is the all-knowing, all-loving Teacher who shows us the way.

VINE

IN TEN WORDS OR LESS
Our spiritual nourishment and growth come only through Jesus.

DETAILS, PLEASE
This is the last of seven "I am" statements of Jesus recorded by the apostle John. By saying "I am the vine, ye are the branches" (John 15:5), Jesus told His original disciples (and, by extension, everyone who would ultimately follow Him) that they needed to stay connected to Him to have any hope of success. As the rest of John 15:5 says, "without me ye can do nothing." Just as a grapevine carries vital nourishment to its branches, allowing bunches of good fruit to grow, so Jesus fills our lives with His strength and goodness, causing us to develop spiritual fruit—love, joy, peace, patience, kindness, goodness, and the like (Galatians 5:22–23).

ADDITIONAL SCRIPTURES
- I am the true vine, and my Father is the husbandman (John 15:1).

- Abide in me, and I in you. As the branch cannot bear fruit of itself, except it abide in the vine; no more can ye, except ye abide in me (John 15:4).

WHAT OTHERS SAY
Whatever life there is in the branch, it flows out of the stem; whatever strength there is in the branch, it comes from its union with the stem; whatever foliage, whatever fruit, all come still out of its union with the stem. And this is the case, whether the branch be great or small. *J. C. Philpot*

SO WHAT?
We don't have to press and strain to create our own spiritual fruit—it's simply a matter of staying close and connected to Jesus, the Vine.

The Way, the Truth, and the Life

In Ten Words or Less
Jesus is the only real path to life.

Details, Please
Jesus used this three-part name for Himself in a conversation with Thomas. The Lord had just told the disciples that His "Father's house" had "many mansions" (*rooms*, NIV; John 14:2), and that He was going there to prepare a place for them. Addressing Thomas's confusion, Jesus said, "I am the way, the truth, and the life: no man cometh unto the Father, but by me" (John 14:6). Note the definite article *the* before each element of this name—Jesus was calling Himself the *only* way, truth, and life. This exclusive claim supports related comments of both Jesus and New Testament leaders (see below).

Additional Scriptures
- I and my Father are one. (John 10:30)

- He that hath seen me hath seen the Father. (John 14:9)

- And this is life eternal, that they might know thee the only true God, and Jesus Christ, whom thou hast sent. (John 17:3)

- Let all the house of Israel know assuredly, that God hath made the same Jesus, whom ye have crucified, both Lord and Christ. (Acts 2:36)

- For there is one God, and one mediator between God and men, the man Christ Jesus. (1 Timothy 2:5)

What Others Say
Jesus makes a no-doubt statement about His position and role in God's redemptive story. "I'm the only shot you've got," He is essentially saying. We like choices, but when it comes to our redemption, Jesus doesn't give us any. *John C. Richards*

So What?
Now that you know Jesus' exclusive claim, you have a choice to make: accept or reject Him.

WORD

IN TEN WORDS OR LESS
Jesus is the full expression of God's mind and thinking.

DETAILS, PLEASE
Just as words allow us to understand another person, "the Word," Jesus, allows us to comprehend God—at least, as far as our limited human minds can. Coming from the Greek term *logos*, indicating "'the expression of thought,' not the mere name of an object" (*Vine's Expository Dictionary of New Testament Words*), "the Word" was a favorite phrase of John, who began both his Gospel and his first letter with it: "In the beginning was the Word, and the Word was with God, and the Word was God" (John 1:1); "That which was from the beginning, which we have heard, which we have seen with our eyes, which we have looked upon, and our hands have handled, of the Word of life. . ." (1 John 1:1). John wanted people to know that Jesus, though God, was also a real human being: "And the Word was made flesh, and dwelt among us, (and we beheld his glory, the glory as of the only begotten of the Father,) full of grace and truth" (John 1:14).

ADDITIONAL SCRIPTURES
- I saw heaven opened, and behold a white horse; and he that sat upon him was called Faithful and True. . . . And he was clothed with a vesture dipped in blood: and his name is called The Word of God. (Revelation 19:11, 13)

WHAT OTHERS SAY
A "word" is that by which we communicate our will; by which we convey our thoughts; or by which we issue commands. The Son of God may be called "the Word," because He is the medium by which God promulgates His will and issues His commandments. *Albert Barnes*

SO WHAT?
God is knowable—through His Word, Jesus Christ.